Intentional Ini_____

As the world changes, how do we educate differently so students, teachers, and staff are empowered to thrive in this environment? In this new book from bestselling author A.J. Juliani, you'll learn a clear process to guide risk-taking and lead change so you can be intentional about innovation in your classroom, school, and life. Juliani shows why we need intentional innovation and how to implement it effectively using the PLASMA framework:

- What to **P**raise, **L**ook For, and **A**ssess
- **S**upport What is Different
- **M**ake Time for Creative Work
- **A**llow for the New and Unknown

You'll also gain insights on celebrating failing and learning, creating conditions for creativity, and leading the change. Whether you are a technology and innovation coach, a teacher, or an administrator, *Intentional Innovation* will motivate you to take risks, be up to date on the latest research, and manage strong working relationships designed to help students succeed beyond school doors. It's not just about technology for change, but about fostering relationships to motivate, inspire, and challenge us to step out and lead in a future that is exciting and unknown.

A.J. Juliani is a leading educator in the area of innovation, design thinking, and inquiry-based learning. Juliani has worked as a Middle and High School English Teacher, a K-12 Technology Staff Developer, an educational consultant for ISTE, and an educational speaker. A.J. is currently the Director of Technology and Innovation for Centennial School District. He is the author of books centered around student-agency, choice, innovative learning, and engagement. As a parent of four young children, A.J. believes we must be intentional about innovation in order to create a better future of learning for all of our students. You can connect with A.J. on his blog, "Intentional Innovation" (located at ajjuliani.com), or through Twitter (@ajjuliani).

Intentional Innovation

How to Guide Risk-Taking, Build Creative Capacity, and Lead Change

A.J. Juliani

Routledge
Taylor & Francis Group

NEW YORK AND LONDON

First published 2018
by Routledge
711 Third Avenue, New York, NY 10017

and by Routledge
2 Park Square, Milton Park, Abingdon, Oxon, OX14 4RN

Routledge is an imprint of the Taylor & Francis Group, an informa business

Library of Congress Cataloging in Publication Data
Names: Juliani, A. J., author.
Title: Intentional innovation : how to guide risk-taking, build creative
    capacity, and lead change / by A.J. Juliani.
Description: New York, NY : Routledge, 2017.
Identifiers: LCCN 2017015836| ISBN 9781138639317 (hardback) |
    ISBN 9781138639324 (pbk.) | ISBN 9781315637266 (ebk.)
Subjects: LCSH: Educational innovations. | Educational leadership. |
    Educational change.
Classification: LCC LB1027 .J85 2017 | DDC 370—dc23
LC record available at https://lccn.loc.gov/2017015836

ISBN: 978-1-138-63931-7 (hbk)
ISBN: 978-1-138-63932-4 (pbk)
ISBN: 978-1-315-63726-6 (ebk)

Typeset in Palatino
by Swales & Willis Ltd, Exeter, Devon, UK

Visit the eResources: www.routledge.com/9781138639324

Contents

eResource: Free Study Guide!

The book comes with a free study guide so you can extend your learning and discuss the ideas with others in PLCs and book groups. You can access it by visiting the book product page: www.routledge.com/9781138639324. Click on the tab that says "eResource" and select the file. It will begin downloading to your computer.

Meet the Author

A.J. Juliani is a leading educator in the area of innovation, design thinking, and inquiry-based learning. Juliani has worked as a Middle and High School English Teacher; a K-12 Technology Staff Developer; an educational consultant for ISTE; and an educational speaker. A.J. is currently the Director of Technology and Innovation for Centennial School District. He is the author of books centered around student-agency, choice, innovative learning, and engagement. As a parent of four young children, A.J. believes we must be intentional about innovation in order to create a better future of learning for all of our students. You can connect with A.J. on his blog, "Intentional Innovation" (located at ajjuliani.com), or through Twitter (@ajjuliani).

A.J. lives in suburban Philadelphia with his wife and four children. He has spent time working in Guatemala with Food for the Hungry, as well as South Africa and Swaziland working with the non-profit Swaziland Relief. More than anything, A.J. is someone who truly believes in the "inquiry-driven" education movement. He wants his kids to grow up in a world that values their ideas.

Introduction

The year was 2007. I was a relatively new teacher and even "newer" to the online world of learning.

I was not tweeting or blogging.

I was Googling. In fact, I was a ferocious Googler of information at this time; always trying to get resources and ideas for my classroom that would inspire and challenge my students.

I was also naïve. And I still believe I'm naïve today (more on that later). But I had no real idea of what the world of information and learning looked like beyond my own experiences. This was before I had read any books about learning/education/teaching, and way before I was reading blogs and articles from colleagues and teachers online.

And then it happened.

I'm not sure how it happened, or how I stumbled across this video. My best guess is a series of Google searches that led me to a rabbit hole of hyper-links through the web until I was stopped cold in my tracks.

I clicked the video and could not stop watching.

My mouth grew wider and wider with each passing clip. And in my head I could only think, if this is true, then what is going on in our world?

Jobs were changing at a faster pace than ever before. More people were online and connected. The world was exponentially innovating, and it was hard to fathom what would change in the next 5, 10, or 15 years!

The video was *Did You Know; Shift Happens* and was created by Karl Fisch and Scott McLeod.[1] And it was this video that changed me.

How Did a Video Change Me?

It's funny to say that a video changed me, but it did. It changed my perspective on what was happening all around me. It changed my perspective on what was important to my students. But most of all, it changed my perspective on what my job was as a teacher.

This quote from the video really hit home on figuring out not only what my role was as a teacher, but also what the role is of educational institutions:

> *We are currently preparing students for jobs that don't yet exist, using technologies that haven't been invented, in order to solve problems we don't even know are problems yet.*
>
> —Karl Fisch

The video sparked my curiosity and led me to:

◆ Get my Master's in Global and International Education;
◆ Read *The World is Flat* by Thomas Friedman and join the "Flat Classroom Project" with my students;
◆ Create Project: Global Inform[2] with students and the 2030Schools[3] projects;
◆ Spend a ton of time connecting with teachers online from around the world; and
◆ Read, read, and read some more about what is happening in our world.

I Asked the Question: If We Don't Know What the Future Is Going to Look Like, Then How Can We Possibly "Prepare" Students?

This is apparent in my own life. My last two jobs as K-12 Technology Staff Developer and Education and Technology Innovation Specialist did not exist when I was in High School. My current job of Director of Technology and Innovation most likely did not exist either.

My teachers could not have possibly "prepared" me for these roles. None of my formal education had anything to do with "technology" either; it was all embedded into what I was doing in my daily life and classroom.

And then I had kids.

My interest in the future of learning grew exponentially when I had kids. When you look at your own children and realize that you have no idea what the world will look like in ten years, it can give you serious anxiety and heartburn (we call this "agita" in my house).

Now, years later, I'm asking the same questions.

How much has changed? How much will change? And what does it mean for us as teachers and learners?

Just look at how business has been transformed by companies in the past five years:

Figure 0.1

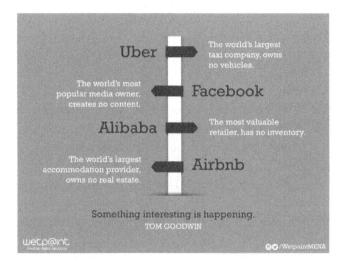

Something interesting *is* happening. It has been happening. And it is going to continue happening. How this exponential change is impacting learning is what I'm really interested in looking at, and diving into as a topic. But this is going to be a tough task, and I'm going to need your help along the way.

The Problem with Most Future of Education and Education Reform Strategies

I think it is important to reason from first principles rather than by analogy. The normal way we conduct our lives is we reason by analogy. [When reasoning by analogy] we are doing this because it's like something else that was done or it is like what other people are doing—slight iterations on a theme.

First principles is kind of a physics way of looking at the world. You boil things down to the most fundamental truths and say, "What are we sure is true?" . . . and then reason up from there.

Somebody could say, "Battery packs are really expensive and that's just the way they will always be . . . Historically, it has cost $600 per kilowatt hour. It's not going to be much better than that in the future".

With first principles, you say, "What are the material constituents of the batteries? What is the stock market value of the material constituents?"

It's got cobalt, nickel, aluminum, carbon, some polymers for separation and a seal can. Break that down on a material basis and say, "If we bought that on the London Metal Exchange what would each of those things cost?"

It's like $80 per kilowatt hour. So clearly you just need to think of clever ways to take those materials and combine them into the shape of a battery cell and you can have batteries that are much, much cheaper than anyone realizes.

—Elon Musk, Founder of SpaceX, CEO of Tesla

In thinking about how we can reform education to *learn better* and how we can *educate better* (or *differently*) I see a lot of people attacking the questions from their own experiences, what companies are doing to be innovative, and what technologies have disrupted other fields and sectors.

Ask yourself this question: what is the last invention that was created solely for the purpose of learning? The last invention that was made for education?

First principles thinking brings us back to asking questions like:

◆ How do we learn best?
◆ Why do we learn?
◆ How is learning changing? Why does it need to change?
◆ How can we teach and guide the learning process in the best possible way?

That is where we need to start. It's where we all need to start to fully immerse ourselves in the question of whether or not education needs to change.

In the next few chapters I'm going to be exploring these questions by answering these questions:

◆ Do we need to educate better?
◆ Do we need to educate differently?
◆ Do we need education (in its current form) at all?

I do not have all the answers. But I want to explore the possibilities. I want to look at the research, trends, and ideas that are disrupting learning right now, and potentially impacting our educational system for years to come.

I believe we need to take a *first principles* approach to discussing our current educational system and how we can learn better—not only in the future, but also right now.

This book dives into a framework for not only dealing with change in the world, but empowering students, teachers, and staff to thrive in this environment.

After we explore how to guide risk-taking and lead change, we'll finish with a clear process, filled with examples to be intentional about innovation in your classroom, school, and life.

At the core of this book is a focus on what has always impacted teaching, learning, making, and creating: our relationships.

As people, we thrive on human and social connections to make sense of the world around us. Technology and change can often lead people to think that relationships may have lost their place. In this book we argue the exact opposite, as relationships are what motivate, inspire, and challenge us to step out and lead in a future that is exciting and unknown.

We Are All Leaders

This book is meant for leaders. Yet, I do not want to separate administrators, teachers, staff, students, and parents into categories. Every person in a school has a capacity to be a leader. Every human can impact others around them in positive, inspiring, and motivational ways.

What I'm hoping is that we can all lead by our actions and attitude: actions that lead by example, showcase resiliency, and implore others to lead; attitude that is of contagious optimism, allowing others around us to get excited about the new and unknown.

Sadly, one of the most recognized "leaders" in our modern era is someone who failed to embody many of these qualities, and has left many folks trying to lead, confused about their role. I have a simple message to those leading in education today.

Stop Trying to Lead Like Steve Jobs

Yes, I said it. I'm talking about the great Steve Jobs, who helped to revolutionize modern communication, phones, computers, personal devices, music (iTunes), animation (Pixar), and many other industries.

Problem is, he was an awful example of what being a leader is all about.

Well, at least his public portrayal as a leader is completely misleading.

You don't have to be an arrogant, overbearing, and demeaning drill sergeant in order to make an impact as a leader.

You don't have to challenge the emotional and social well-being of individuals on your team to get the "best work" out of them.

✦ You don't have to burn bridges and put personal relationships on the back-burner in order to be a great leader.

In fact, I'd argue that Steve Jobs was effective despite these qualities. The man was innovative, his company extremely profitable, and he continually pushed ideas out to the world with empathy for the customer's life and experience.

Yet, many people (me included) missed the true genius of Steve Jobs' leadership. It wasn't about the fiery arguments, tight deadlines, and overbearing attention to details.

Jobs did something quite unique. He allowed for new and innovative ideas to permeate Apple's culture. He made time for conversations and iterations in the design process, even if it put off launching a product when it was supposed to be ready. He supported new ways of thinking, marketing, and product development. And best of all, he praised creative work, looked for people who thought differently, and assessed his company beyond just revenue and sales.

All of that gets lost in some of the recent articles and movies about Jobs' life. Let's keep it real. He doesn't seem like the best person to work for, and especially work under. His management antics that have received the most publicity are ones that no leader should aspire to.

But, underneath the brash and unapologetic characterization of Jobs is a compelling case of what pushes innovation out of pockets and into a culture.

Innovation Does Not Have a Finish Line

Jobs is a great example of not only the many faces of leadership, but also the many ways in which innovation is misunderstood by our institutions.

Innovation, it seems, does not have a finish line. It is never done, finished, or complete. There is always another iteration, a new problem to solve, and a fresh way of thinking that the world needs.

This book is meant to be a piece to the puzzle. As someone who has seen education from a variety of roles (student, teacher, administrator, professor, and parent), I realize the work to transform teaching and learning is never done, and it looks different depending on the area, school, classroom, and student. I do not (nor wish to) offer a prescription of "how to innovate", but instead want to focus on looking at the factors, stories, and research that surround innovative learning.

This is your idea. But it may also be our idea, or their idea, or an old idea. Your job is to make it work. Your job is to fail as many times as you need to before this idea becomes a reality.

That is innovation.

Ideas that work.

But be careful. Always ask, who does this idea work for? Who does it help? Who could it harm? How may it make the world a better place?

Innovation is neither inherently good nor evil. Yet, your intentions matter.

Be intentional in innovation, both in process and purpose. Intentional in what you allow for and make time for, in order to foster innovative work.

Intentional in what you praise, look for, and ultimately assess as an idea worthy of your time and our time.

Intentional purpose may not always lead to your desired results, but it will keep you on the path of innovating for a true belief.

Intentional innovation is therefore a process that an individual, or group, goes through to find a way for new ideas to work.

The process might look different whether you are in a business, classroom, or laboratory, but the intentions are similar.

We innovate to make the world a better place. So be intentional in your actions to that end.

Notes

1 I'm sure many of you have seen either this original, or one of the other versions (version 2.0, version 3.0, version 4.0, version 5.0). See http://ajjuliani.com/shift.
2 http://ajjuliani.com/project-global-inform-doing-something-about-human-rights-violations.
3 http://ajjuliani.com/lets-change-the-world-with-our-students-heres-how.

Part 1

The Need for Innovation

1

The Unlearning Cycle

My parents took our family on a trip to Maine to ski when I was in my early teens. We went to visit friends and this was way out of our comfort zone. My family was much more likely to take a trip down to the beach than the mountains. And I had only gone skiing a few times, before we decided to risk our lives on the Maine powder.

The mountains there are much bigger than what we were used to in Pennsylvania, and I was not ready to ski those slopes. I was a bit scared to do anything but put my skis in a wedge (pizza style) and slow-mo my way down the mountain.

My dad (not the best skier either) told me a story about his first time skiing. He was a city boy growing up, who didn't get the opportunity to learn how to ski until he was leading a group of teenagers on a trip to a local mountain. It took him a while to tie the skis to his boots (this was before the fancy click-in skis we have today) and he headed to the ski lift to get carried up to the top.

He explained how he watched the ski lift pass a couple of times before he got the hang of how to catch it at the right moment (if you've ever been skiing, you'll know this a critical skill). Then, as he stepped onto the lift platform—BOOM—it hit his leg and he half-slid onto the seat as it began to rise up into the sky.

Unaware of the bar to pull over your head, my dad grabbed the side of the lift-chair, holding on for dear life. He looked around. No one noticed him struggling. As he regained composure and sat upright in the chair he realized that the tie on his left ski had been undone and it was hanging by a thread on his boot. Then, he looked ahead and saw where he would have to get off the lift. Instantly, thoughts began to fill his head. *What if I came off the lift and broke my ankle? What if I fell and slid down, unable to control where I landed?* He scanned the area and came up with a plan: he was going to jump off the chair onto one of the big metal poles holding up the lift!

As he began to rock back and forth in his chair, people below took notice. What was that man doing in the chair? Why was he rocking so hard without his bar placed in front? What was he going to do?

His group of teenagers also saw what was happening, but it was too late. My dad timed the rocking to a point where he jumped off the chair and onto a big pole. The crowd gasped. He slid down the pole, skis still on his feet, until he landed on the snow below. Immediately, people rushed to his rescue, but as they got close all they could hear was him laughing . . . at that moment, he had finally realized how ridiculous he must have looked jumping off the ski lift!

Learning and Unlearning

The story made me feel better about my awkwardness as a beginner skier, and it still speaks to me years later. When we learn something new we often have a pretty picture in our head of what that is going to look like. Yet, in reality it often looks something like this:

Figure 1.1

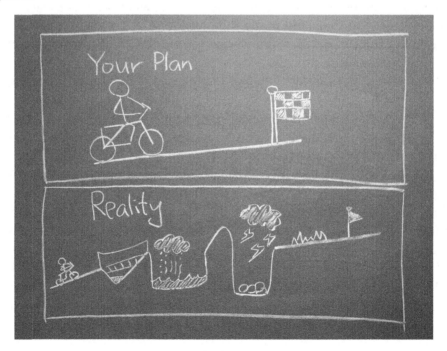

Learning something new can be exciting and exhilarating, but it can also be tiring and frustrating. In my dad's case, it can also be embarrassing. But I don't believe that is just limited to his skiing story.

How many times have you personally not given your best (100%) effort to learn and try something new because you'd look like a fool and could potentially embarrass yourself?

> *Don't fear failure so much that you refuse to try new things. The saddest summary of a life contains three descriptions: could have, might have, and should have.*
>
> —Louis E. Boone

I'd like to call myself a risk-taker, but guess what? I spent five years in a band around musicians who could play multiple instruments and I never learned how to play guitar, or the drums, or the piano. I spent countless hours writing lyrics, but was too scared to really spend time learning an instrument. Want to know why? I had bad experiences. Whether it was the trumpet in 5th grade, or the piano at my house, I categorized myself as someone who could never learn an instrument.

I would play the guitar (*concrete experience*), have little to no success (*reflective observation*), and then conclude I was bad at playing the guitar, and would never get any better (*abstract conceptualization*). So, *active experimentation* never truly happened because I'd already pegged myself at a certain skill level.

Does this sound like you at all? Does it sound like any students in your class? Does it sound like any of your children?

Figure 1.2

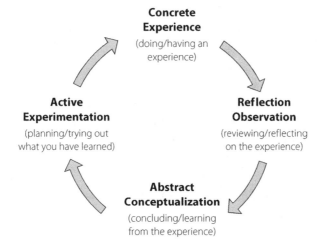

Figure 1.3

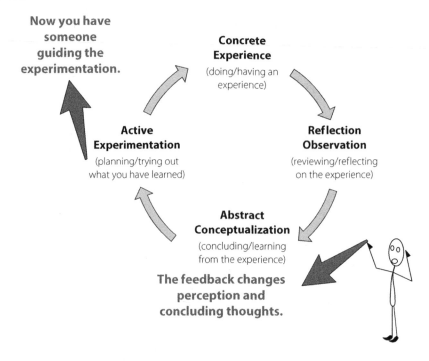

Learning changes with a teacher/guide/mentor. Teachers inspire, challenge, and help push learners to active experimentation, even when we as learners aren't sure about our perceived skills.

I see this all the time with my own kids. Whether they are learning to ride a bike, talk for the first time, or understanding the basics of math, feedback is critical to their learning process.

But what does it look like when you've hit success in all of these areas, and then are suddenly told you need to change and learn something new?

What if you've stopped the *active experimentation* piece of the cycle, because for years and years the feedback you received is that you've mastered this skill already?

And what if that "years and years" part has changed to "months and months" and "days and days" in the past few decades? What if every time you learned something new and thought you had a solid understanding, it changed? What if this happened repeatedly in all different situations in your life?

Sounds frustrating, right?!

But that's what is happening right now. It's why "learning" has changed, and how "unlearning" is the key to a radical revolution in the future of education.

Unlearning Throughout History . . .

I remember coming back home from an elementary school lesson and telling my parents that people actually thought the world was flat, and the Earth was the center of the solar system.

And yet, each generation has had beliefs that were later proven to be completely wrong (or misguided) and indefensible, in light of new information or scientific discoveries.

Let's take the "Earth as the center of the solar system" example. Europeans were basically using the old Greek beliefs of the solar system. Some people questioned these beliefs, but they played perfectly into the religion, culture, and science of the time. There were problems with the theory, but if no one actually believes it is a theory (and rather believes it to be pure truth), then it is extremely difficult to disprove.

Copernicus comes around and drops a knowledge bomb on the entire world (while on his deathbed) when he publishes a book supporting his "Sun as the center of the solar system" theory (let's finally call it heliocentric) in 1543. Well, no one believes him. They call it heresy. And most people go about their business the same as before.

By 1650, most astronomers (thanks to Galileo's efforts) believed the science supported the heliocentric view on the world, and helped persuade the public on the validity of this theory.

We Can Look at This Through Two Different Learning Lenses

First, most of this learning was done out of interest, not necessarily necessity. Columbus was crossing the Atlantic using the old view of astronomy, finding new worlds and stuff. So, most people thought they were smart enough to go anywhere and do anything with their current belief system about the stars. We've seen other seismic shifts in human thinking come out of necessity, but this (along with many scientific discoveries) came from the human desire to be curious and challenge through interest.

Second, look how long it actually took for a theory that was completely justifiable to be accepted by the general public: over 100 years!

So, as humans, we've always had to unlearn. Whether (as happened recently in my house) that is my young son touching a cold stove top one day and believing it is ok to touch, and then hitting it again the next day when it is on and hot, and realizing it is not ok to touch. Or it may be scientific discoveries or theories that we accept and therefore unlearn a past practice or belief.

We've always improved through unlearning and relearning, although the unlearning used to have a longer curve to it. In fact, we've seen social unlearning (think cigarette smoking) struggle to happen quickly, compared to pure scientific unlearning.

What Does This Mean To Us As Teachers, Parents, and Learners?

Well, it means we have to unlearn and relearn at a much more frequent pace than generations before us, and this pace will increase in the coming years and generations.

When you are at work, or at home, and think that you cannot simply handle one more change . . . sorry . . . the changes won't stop, they are going to keep coming in waves, and there is not much you or I or anyone can do about it.

Pace of Exponential Change

The video I mentioned in the introduction (*Did You Know; Shift Happens*)[1] has been revised and updated numerous times since it first came out eight years ago. One of the facts from that video that struck me as crazy was the pace of exponential change.

And not only is our knowledge doubling at a rapid rate, but also the amount of data is growing exponentially. Look at this chart depicting how much data we are currently dealing with:

Figure 1.4

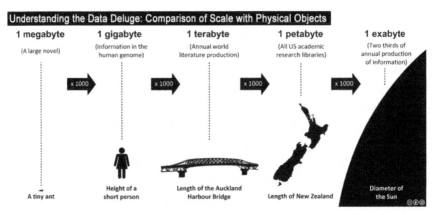

If the research, observations, and data are even close to being correct in their understanding and predictions, then we are going to have to get ready to do a whole lot more unlearning in the very near future (like right now).

It also means that our ideas of what learning looks like are going to have to change. And it starts with accepting and embracing the unlearning cycle.

The Unlearning Cycle

When looking at *why we learn* it can usually be boiled down to two reasons: interest and necessity, both of which are tied to attention. These two reasons take various different forms (survival is a form of necessity) and can be interchanged with other terms—curiosity is similar to interest—but if you think about your life and what you have learned, it usually comes down to things you *had to learn* and things you *wanted to learn.*

The part of all this that is mind boggling to me is that for centuries and centuries the *necessity* part of learning slowed down as you aged. The world wasn't changing that rapidly, and as you became an adult there wasn't much forcing you to learn—although I'd have to say my kids have forced me to relearn a lot. Sure, there were always new learning experiences to be had, but the unlearning didn't happen like it does today.

My dad (who still can't ski) has had to unlearn and relearn seven different cell phones in the past 12 years! He's had to unlearn modes of communication and relearn how to communicate with his family and friends. It seems like each holiday season he's getting a new technology in his hands that makes him unlearn what he learned the previous season. He just found out what a Snapchat story is because he *wants* to see all the pictures and videos of his grandkids, and he has to keep up. His life at 63 years old is filled with monthly and daily unlearning occurrences, and he is relearning at a faster and faster pace each year.

The real kicker is that most of his unlearning and relearning experiences are coming out of necessity, not out of interest.

Our Learning Bias

> *Truth is truth, no matter what I think about it. So be very careful how you interpret things, because you're looking at the world with a bias whether you think you are or not.*
>
> —Destin at SmarterEveryDay

We are looking at the world through a bias. Our bias includes our experiences, our upbringing, and our environment. We have many biases around the ideas of learning. Most of us have experienced a similar type of schooling between the ages of 5–18. We believe that because "we turned out alright" that this same type of learning experience is not only good for our kids, but there is no reason to change it.

The truth is that when you look at our learning from a *first principles* perspective, a lot has changed. A lot is going to change. And learning is no longer a linear process. It is one where we have to take steps to the side, and steps backward, in order to relearn and recalibrate our biases, beliefs, and understanding of the world and what will work.

What we know though is that people believe (across many cultures and ages) that change is bad, very bad:

> *It's not just that people fear change, though they undoubtedly do. It's also that they genuinely believe (often on an unconscious level) that when you've been doing something a particular way for some time, it must be a good way to do things. And the longer you've been doing it that way, the better it is. So change isn't simply about embracing something unknown—it's about giving up something old (and therefore good) for something new (and there-fore not good).*[2]

A study[3] in November 2000 shows that people have a very reliable and tangible preference for things that have been around longer. In one study, students preferred the course requirement described as the status quo over a new version, (regardless of whether the new version meant more *or* less coursework), and liked it even more when it had been around for 100 years, rather than only 10 years.

How do you view change? Do you accept that the world is changing, or continue along with the same biases towards learning and education?

Hopefully your answer to that question now is, "Yes, I get it A.J.! The world is changing at a rapid pace and I have to embrace this idea of unlearn-ing and relearning!"

Maybe you don't need to yell that from the mountaintops. But, if you are a teacher, leader, or parent, it's important to acknowledge that we are going to have to learn, unlearn, and relearn as much (or maybe even more) than our students and children do.

Deeper learning requires connecting old and new knowledge in initially unfamiliar ways. While *knowledge* is an indicator of what infor-mation we have access to, *understanding* indicates what connections we are able to make between one bit of knowledge and another. According to

Understanding by Design by Wiggins and McTighe, "Misunderstanding is not ignorance, therefore. It is the mapping of a working idea in a plausible but incorrect way in a new situation."

Unlearning Has to Be Followed by Relearning

Here are the steps that we take:

1. An interest or necessity (with excitement or urgency) leads to *learning*.
2. An interest or necessity (with resistance and/or urgency) leads to *unlearning*.
3. An interest or necessity (with excitement or urgency) leads us to *relearn*.

My question then is: do we allow for this process in our schools, and do we promote this process in our schools?

Bring It Back to the Basics

These chapters are about answering the question: does education really need to change? We want to do this from a *first principles* perspective in which we dive into why we learn, how we learn, and whether those reasons are changing—or need to change.

We've always been learners, and it is innately human to want to learn. But, what we've seen is that we have always been unlearners as well. Unlearning has been as important a process to our growth as any other factor.

The problem is that unlearning is hard. It rails against our biases. It takes our feedback and turns it upside down. It makes successful people fight for things to stay the same. And it makes even the most forward-thinking individuals question whether or not the process is worth it . . .

The implications for school are even more important. If our exponential change curve has unlearning and relearning happening at a much faster and faster rate, then consider this:

◆ Most curriculum cycles in schools are longer than five years.
◆ Many students don't get a chance to retake assessments or redo work (no unlearning allowed!).

- Schools create K-12 scope and sequences for specific content (most which will be outdated by the time students are in 4th grade).
- Students are often forced to "pick" a career path and major before they even graduate high school.
- Countless professions have one or two tests that "certify" individuals without testing their skills or abilities when the world (and their profession) changes.

The list can go on and on. We are living in a world of exponential growth that still uses fixed measures.

Education needs to not only look to what the future is going to be, in order to better teach and learn; but also look in the mirror to acknowledge the realities of our current learning environment. Let's celebrate unlearning in our schools and classrooms, and find more ways to make relearning a daily practice that we support and promote.

Notes

1 http://ajjuliani.com/education-change.
2 www.huffingtonpost.com/heidi-grant-halvorson-phd/why-we-dont-like-change_b_1072702.html.
3 https://doi.org/10.1016/j.jesp.2010.07.008.

Chapter Reflection

What ideas resonated with you from this chapter? Take notes, draw, brainstorm, and reflect in the space below. Share your ideas on Twitter using the hashtag #beintentional.

2

The Science Behind Learning

One day, I peeked over the shoulder of a student in the library. She was quietly working, with headphones in and completely focused. What caught my attention is that she would continually lift her phone up over her textbook, and then jot something down on the paper to her left. It was a motion and process that she repeated at least seven times before I headed over to see what was going on.

As I got closer I could see that it was a math textbook, and her paper was filled with equations, problems, and steps. That sure doesn't look like my math homework did, I thought to myself; mine was always a mess of numbers, lines, and eraser marks from messing up!

What happened next caught me by surprise. Not because I couldn't believe it, but because it changed the way I viewed math forever.

The student would pick up her iPhone (or maybe it was an Android) and open up an app. Then, flicking over to a clear screen, she would hover the phone over a specific problem in her textbook.

What happened next was nothing short of magic. If, per chance, someone had been transported here from even 20 years ago they might not have believed it was possible.

The phone immediately (I mean, it was quick!) overlaid the problem with multiple steps and a solution, all in a row on her screen. She jotted down the answers on her piece of paper and moved on to the next problem.

I, on the other hand, had to first stop my mouth from dropping, then I tapped her on the shoulder.

She was startled, and took out one headphone.

"What is that?" I questioned.

"Oh, it's PhotoMath. It's an app."

"Are you allowed to use that? Is it something your teacher uses in class?"

"Um, I don't think Ms. Carter knows about it, but no one ever said we couldn't use it. Am I in trouble?"

I told her she wasn't in trouble at all and continued to ask a few more questions about how the app worked. But there wasn't much to learn. It worked just as I saw it work. I quickly Googled the app on my own phone and found a video, which is eerily similar to what I saw in the library that day.

We tend to hear stories all the time of computers doing "human things" and impacting productivity—but this time it was different: this time I saw a direct connection between a technology and how it could eliminate the need to learn something (more on that later).

In 1997 it was Deep Blue taking down Gary Kasparov in a chess match, where the cognitive ability of computers finally ascended to the level of a human's, and beyond. By 2005 there were no chess champions that could even try and compete with the chess-playing computers.

Now, computers (in 2017) can learn to play and master video games—like Atari's Pong—with no guidance at all from a human. And we've seen Artificial Intelligence grow to new levels.

But still, none of these abilities impacted or affected learning on a student level. It was stuff we would only hear about in the news. They did not change the basic ways that we learn something new. Because in order for learning to change, it has to affect one of the four stages of how we actually learn something.

The Four Stages to Actually Learning Something

The blessing and the curse is that over the past 10–20 years there have been numerous books, articles, and videos centered around the idea of cognitive science—or the science of *how* we learn.

Still, during my research, many of those books and videos focused on one specific stage of the learning process, and did not give a full overview of what it looked like to not know something, to know something, and then be able to use that knowledge and understanding in the real world.

This, to me, is one of the most important pieces of information an educator can have. It should be the foundation to our practice. **If we want to teach to the best of our abilities, we should have a clear understanding of how our students learn, and what helps them learn best.**

But we tend to only hit the science of learning in one (maybe two) undergraduate courses, before losing much of that information by the time we actually start working with students. It is rarely brought up in professional development. I have almost never seen it mentioned at the numerous education conferences around the world. And, when I've asked the question to teachers and leaders, most don't have a clear understanding of how we actually learn.

To be honest. Neither did I.

It wasn't that I didn't care; I did—and still do. It's that I was filling my mind with all other types of information relating to teaching and learning, without starting with the *first principles* of why we learn and how we learn.

Here is Peter Nilsson describing the four stages to learning on his blog, Sense and Sensation:[1]

Figure 2.1

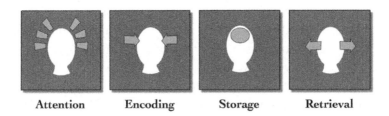

How People Learn:

Four Cognitive Processes Every Teacher Should Know

Attention   Encoding   Storage   Retrieval

senseandsensation.com

So how do people learn? What are the mechanics of memory? Can we distill thousands of articles and books to something that is manageable, digestible, and applicable to our classrooms?

Yes. In brief, the cognitive process of learning has four basic stages:

1. Attention: the filter through which we experience the world.
2. Encoding: how we process what our attention admits into the mind.
3. Storage: what happens once information enters the brain.
4. Retrieval: the recall of that information or behavior.

Almost everything we do or know, we learn through these stages, for our learning is memory, and the bulk of our memory is influenced by these four processes: what we pay attention to, how we encode it, what happens to it in storage, and when and how we retrieve it.

Let's start with *attention*. Going back to the previous chapter on why we learn,[2] it all begins with attention. Most of the time we pay attention for two reasons: interest or necessity.

Our brain is flooded with information from a multi-sensory world that is throwing sounds, sights, feelings, and everything else at us in rapid succession. With all of this information coming at us we tend to pay attention to things that we are curious about and interested in, or information that has a direct correlation to our physical, emotional, or psychological well-being.

Then comes the *encoding*. Our senses are being hit with so much information, that when we finally process that information we begin to categorize it as a new experience or a connected experience with prior knowledge.

After we've successfully paid attention and made some connections—or created new information—we come to the *storage* stage. Here, we store this new or connected information in our short-term, working, or long-term memory. Where it is stored and how it is stored is associated with how powerful the experience is/was, and how often we bring that experience back into our daily lives.

Retrieval is the final stage. This is when we pull information out of the memory to help us in learning something new, adapting to a situation, or connecting the dots on an experience. Retrieval also allows us to "re-encode", which starts the learning process all over again: it's like a mini-version of the unlearning/relearning cycle we discussed in the last chapter.

You can think about how this cycle of learning works in all different types of contexts and experiences. From real world applications, like driving a car, to classroom situations, like understanding photosynthesis, the more we retrieve information and connect it to new experiences, the stronger our understanding becomes around that topic and idea.

This is why most of you reading this chapter have a better sense of how to drive a car than how photosynthesis works. Even though photosynthesis happens every day, all around you, it does not impact you; or in other words, it does not grab your attention. Driving a car, on the other hand, is connected to your daily life as an adult for work, pleasure, and all other kinds of reasons.

Our students, just like all of us, tend to prioritize the learning of things that will impact them. It is in our nature to pay attention (and kick off the learning process) to information that is connected to our interests and needs.

So, what happens when technology evolves and takes away some of the need to learn in a few areas? What happens when we retrieve information from other places besides our memory? And, what happens when technology eliminates the need to learn certain information because we'll never need to retrieve it at all?

How Technology Is Impacting the Way Our Brains Work

Consider the fact that technological advances over the years have always impacted how we learn, and changed how we engage with the learning process.

Before the written word/language we could only gather information through oral processes to connect learning experiences. When scrolls and books entered our daily lives, learning could be retrieved through other processes, and our encoding of information was taken to a new level. Similarly, the internet, personal computing devices, and smartphones have begun to revolutionize what we give our attention to, how we encode information, where our new information is stored, and how we go about retrieving and re-encoding what we've learned.

In an article published by *Wired* magazine titled, "How the Web Became Our 'External Brain' and What It Means for Our Kids",[3] author Michael Harris dives into the ways technology is impacting the biology of our brain:

> *The brains our children are born with are not substantively different from the brains our ancestors had 40,000 years ago. For all the wild variety of our cultures, personalities, and thought patterns, we're all still operating with roughly the same three-pound lump of gray matter. But almost from day one, the allotment of neurons in those brains (and therefore the way they function) is different today from the way it was even one generation ago. Every second of your lived experience represents new connections among the roughly 86 billion neurons packed inside your brain. Children, then, can become literally incapable of thinking and feeling the way their grandparents did. A slower, less harried way of thinking may be on the verge of extinction.*
>
> *In your brain, your billions of neurons are tied to each other by trillions of synapses, a portion of which are firing right now, forging (by still mysterious means) your memory of this sentence, your critique of this very notion, and your emotions as you reflect on this information. Our brains are so plastic that they will re-engineer themselves to function optimally in whatever environment we give them. Repetition of stimuli produces a strengthening of responding neural circuits. Neglect of other stimuli will cause corresponding neural circuits to weaken. (Grannies who maintain their crossword puzzle regime knew that already.)*

UCLA's Gary Small is a pioneer of neuroplasticity research, and in 2008 he produced the first solid evidence showing that our brains are reorganized by our use of the internet. He placed a set of 'internet naïve' people in MRI machines and made recordings of their brain activity while they took a stab at going online. Small then had each of them practice browsing the internet for an hour a day for a week. On returning to the MRI machine, those subjects now toted brains that lit up significantly in the frontal lobe, where there had been minimal neural activity beforehand. Neural pathways quickly develop when we give our brains new tasks, and Small had shown that this held true—over the course of just a few hours, in fact—following internet use.

Young people now count on the internet as "their external brain" and have become skillful decision makers—even while they also "thirst for instant gratification and often make quick, shallow choices".

Flash back to the story of the student with the PhotoMath app; we can see technology eliminating some of the ways in which she learns. She was paying attention while doing her math homework. It was mostly created out of necessity (due to grades) but it did start with a form of attention. And then the app took over, giving instant gratification in the form of encoding and retrieving theorems and formulas, and steps to correctly answer the problem.

In the girl's brain, it was the same as copying answers out of the back of the textbook. However, it was better because she did get to see all of the steps in the correct order. This experience still has her attention, but changes the encoding, storage, and retrieval process.

The Question Is Whether or Not We Think This Is OK

Is it OK for students to not know the steps to solving a math problem, but be able to use technology to quickly solve it and use the results for a specific purpose?

Is it OK for students to not know their state capitals because they can ask Siri?

Is it OK for students to not know a language because their device can translate words in real-time while they are listening to or reading it?

And if we don't think it is OK, then what the heck are we going to do about it? It doesn't seem like this issue is going to magically disappear or go away . . .

Technology (if you haven't noticed) is impacting all four stages of learning:

Technology is impacting *attention* through interest and necessity. We live in a world where notifications, vibrations, and messaging drives our thoughts and satisfies our need for instant gratification. We don't have to wait any more for what we want, so attention spans drop and deep work (and a state of flow) is sometimes impossible to do.

Technology is impacting *encoding* in how we connect our current experiences to past experiences. Digital bookmarking and real-time collaboration tools make this process fast, and the scalability even faster. Now the "internet of things" is connecting our experiences to those of others' and we are learning at an exponential pace, doubling our knowledge every 12 months.

Technology is impacting *storage* because our memories now have an external companion. The companion is not a book, or encyclopedia, or library that we have to dive through to find information. Most of this knowledge can be gained by a click of a button or asking a computer voice to reveal it to you.

Technology is impacting *retrieval* because of the very fact that we can retrieve memories/experiences and knowledge from millions of people, categorize them, and put them into the perfect model for retrieval: written, oral, video, etc.

This impact is going to increase with exponential speed and growth over the following years and decades. Technology has always impacted learning, but now it is almost reinventing the notion of what it means to learn, and how we do it.

The SAMR Model Is Missing a Level

The SAMR Model is one of the most pervasive technology integration frameworks for education. It is used by teachers and schools all around the world. Developed by Dr. Putendura, SAMR was a response to looking at technology in education from a transformative perspective. Each "level" on SAMR seeks to identify how the technology can help to enhance and/or transform the learning experience for the student.

The model starts with **S** for **Substitution**. Technology can substitute, but the functionality stays the same. Writing on a chalkboard is the same function as writing on a whiteboard, on an overhead projector, or a smartboard—as long as all you are doing is project words and diagrams.

Figure 2.2

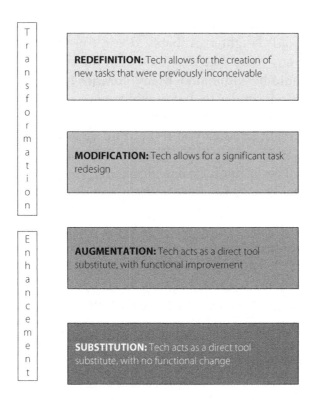

A is for **Augmentation**. Where technology has direct functional improvement over previous methods. This is like writing in a notebook by hand vs. writing in Microsoft Word. The editing, saving, and other tools take the functionality up a notch.

M is for **Modification**. Now we have a scenario where students begin to use Google Docs to write, and have real-time auto-saving and collaboration functionality. It has modified and redesigned the task to allow for new possibilities.

Finally, we have **R** for **Redefinition**. When my students took their Google documents that were collaborated on, and then shared them on a blog with students in Australia and Qatar, it was redefining what was previously possible. Their feedback and collaboration across continents to create a script for a video they would publish and share with thousands of people online, made a learning activity go beyond anything previously inconceivable.

But the SAMR Model is missing a level. It's at the top and is happening to industries, businesses, and schools all over the world at this very moment.

What happens when technology is no longer "integrated" into what we do, but instead "eliminates" what we do because of the advancement?

My six-year-old daughter probably doesn't need to know the Dewey Decimal system any more. She may be taught the system, but many librarians argue it should be eliminated. Many libraries have ditched the system for a BISAC method, similar to that of which you see in big bookstores; but even the days may be numbered for that system.

Augmented reality allows you to hold up your phone—or any device with a camera—and simply tell you where in the library or store a specific book is located. The technology has eliminated the need to learn, memorize, and store the Dewey Decimal system in your memory (as I had to do as a kid).

Even more so, the need for libraries is being eliminated in many colleges, at least in the traditional sense of what a library was. Many of these spaces are being transformed and renovated to have a much different feel and purpose. I spent almost no time in the library as a graduate student and was able to do all of my research online: much quicker and easier to find information through databases.

Technology has proven time and time again that it eliminates many skills previously valued by past generations. You can look at the impact on agriculture (we grow vegetables in the basement of our school). Or look at the impact on transportation (I don't need to know how to ride a horse). Or look at the impact on healthcare (I don't like going to the doctor so no examples for this one!).

Whether we want to embrace it or not, the fact is that technology has transformed our world and the reality of learning, and living, in it.

The science shows that our brains are evolving slowly, while the world around us is evolving quickly.[4] This eliminates the need for many of the learning tasks we previously had to do (i.e. taking notes) and has us rely much more heavily on a third-party teacher: usually not an actual teacher, but instead a machine/device/computer of some sort.

So, **E** is when you get to the top of the SAMR Ladder and get off onto a building or structure. **E** is when you sit in the lifeguard chair at the pool. **Elimination** (via technological advances) is happening all around us, and we can't deny its impact on our world of teaching and learning.

If this sounds "scary" to you, maybe it should be a bit unnerving. **It scares me but also excites me at the same time.**

I think of students, like me when I was in school, that don't "play the game of school" well. I didn't like taking notes, which hurt me when it came time to study for a multiple choice test. I didn't like reading only books that were chosen for me, which hurt when I didn't have a choice in selection. I didn't like doing 50 math problems at night to try and "understand" the concept.

Because technology can help change this game of school: it opens up new opportunities for students who struggle in a traditional setting, to find success in a non-traditional path where other skills are valued and assessed.

And isn't that what this is all about? Isn't this a main purpose of technology in education: to give all students the best chance to learn and succeed?

Which brings up the big question that we are trying to answer: does education really need to change?
First, we need to agree that things are changing now faster than ever before.

This chapter is meant to examine how we learn, and whether or not that four-stage process is also changing. But I think what we've uncovered is the idea that while our brains are changing due to technology, the big shift is the elimination of the types of learning we would do, and how the four stages are being interwoven with our "external brain".

So What Is Actually Changing?

Environment is changing. Our learning environments are shifting away from "places" we go to learn—like a school classroom or library—to an on-demand learning environment where you can have not only access to information at your fingertips, but also access to experts, mentors, and teachers with a click of a button.

Pace is changing. We've seen informational, technological, and artificial intelligence grow at an exponential rate, in which we are creating new technologies and solving new problems that never existed.

Intelligence is changing. It's no longer about what you know, but how fast you can find the knowledge, how well you can use it, and what you can create with it.

Work is changing. Jobs are being destroyed by automation. New jobs are being created by technology. Everyone has to be an innovator, a creator, and a problem solver. Gone are the days of following marching orders and climbing the ladder.

However . . .

Learning is always a social process. It has been and continues to be driven by real human interaction and social connections; even though many of those connections are now happening in an online space.

Learning is always going to be driven by meaning. We learn best when what we are learning is meaningful and relevant to our lives. How can we continue to make it meaningful as our lives change?

Learning follows the four-stage process. It starts with attention and is rebooted by retrieval. We must focus on the *first principles* of learning to harness the beneficial ways technology can help in the teaching/learning process.

What happens if we don't change, but technology keeps changing the world around us?

Consider the following scenario:

We give our students the tests.

Machines grade the tests.

Test data is used to measure the teacher.

The teacher teaches to the test . . .

But what happens when the machine teaches the test, and then grades the test, and the data says the machine is a better teacher than the actual teacher? **We have to focus on teaching above and beyond the test, so our students are empowered to learn deeply, create daily, and inspire each other to dare greatly.**

Let's be intentional about innovation and focus on doing the work that a machine could never do, and technology could never replace.

Notes

1 http://www.senseandsensation.com.
2 http://ajjuliani.com/the-unlearning-cycle-why-we-learn-and-how-its-changing.
3 www.wired.com/2014/08/end-of-absence-how-technology-changes-our-brains-society-children.
4 http://ajjuliani.com/the-science-of-learning-and-technologys-impact-on-how-we-learn.

Chapter Reflection

What ideas resonated with you from this chapter? Take notes, draw, brainstorm, and reflect in the space below. Share your ideas on Twitter using the hashtag #beintentional.

3

Inspiring a Generation of Innovators

It seems that after all this research I've done on the current state of education, and all the reading I've done on the future of learning, one piece of information keeps coming back to get me again and again. It's basically screaming at me when I look at past innovations, past movements and reforms, and current changes in education.

My Opinion on the Future of Education (and Learning) Doesn't Matter

Does that seem harsh? Give me a minute to explain.

I wish that my opinion mattered, I really do. I'm sure you wish your opinion mattered as well. It would help us all feel empowered to go out and change education. But sadly, much of what we talk about online, opinions we share at conferences, and blog posts we write don't actually matter (and by *matter* I mean impact or influence anything).

A few years ago, teachers were angry about the use of cellphones in school. They wanted them banned (some still do). Other teachers fought back, saying students should be allowed to bring their cellphones to school and use them for learning. In both cases, their opinions didn't matter.

Students brought their phones to school regardless of the opinions of adults. Schools made policies on both sides of the debates, and students kept bringing their phones. The phones were a part of their life, a part of what they did, who they were, and how they communicated and connected with the world. The policies educators made didn't matter. The world had already changed, and we couldn't stop it even if we wanted to.

Opinions Tend to Be Reactive, and Reactionary Education Is Not Effective

But, if we learned anything from the previous chapters, it's that the world is changing exponentially, our reasons for learning have been impacted, and the ways in which we learn have been transformed.

So if our opinions don't matter, and we still want to see a better education for our students and children, then what can we do about it?

We can focus our attention on two areas that matter: our attitude and our actions.

As acclaimed author, Thomas Friedman, said in his book *The World is Flat*:

> *The world doesn't care what you know. What the world cares about is what you can do with what you know.*

The world doesn't care about our opinions either. The world only cares about what we are going to do about it, and what our attitude is when we take action.

Action: Schools Like Blockbuster or Netflix?

When I talk with schools I often give this message: we need to think and act like Netflix, not like Blockbuster.

In fact, this is a sentiment I've heard shared over and over by leaders and teachers at educational conferences, in blog posts, and articles on change in schools.

The focus with this analogy is slightly different. Blockbuster had great intentions. Its vision, mission, and focus were clear; none of that needed to change. Instead, it was their actions that led them to a swift demise.

Blockbuster was doing everything right. It had a fantastic business. It was booming and growing each year. It would tweak something here or there: improve customer service; move to DVDs or Blu-ray—but the model stayed the same. Because in all honesty, the model was working.

Figure 3.1

> **"We're strategically better positioned than almost anybody out there.**
> **Never in my wildest dreams would I have aimed this high."**
>
> –Blockbuster's head of digital strategy

Blockbuster focused its attention on providing convenient entertainment, for a cheap cost, in the quickest way possible.

Then Netflix came along and challenged Blockbuster by telling customers they didn't have to go to the store any more. Netflix would send the DVDs right to your house . . . for a monthly flat fee. A lot of people liked this. They could go online, pick out the movies and TV shows to add to their queue, and have a steady flow of DVDs coming in throughout the month.

Blockbuster said, "We can do that too"—but you all know this is not how the story ended.

The interesting piece is that Blockbuster's focus was on point: people will always want cheap, easy, and convenient entertainment.

But the idea of "cheap" went from a $3 rental, to an $8 per month flat fee. The idea of "easy" went from taking a quick drive to the closest store, to clicking a button at home and receiving the movie in your mailbox. The idea of "convenient" changed from popping a DVD into your DVD player into streaming the movie on any device.

Netflix changed its entire business model to meet the growing needs of people who wanted to stream movies and TV shows to their devices. While Blockbuster was left wondering why its model wasn't working.

The difference is simple: Netflix saw how the world was changing around it, and adjusted accordingly. It wasn't doing something "better", instead it was doing something "different" because it matched its offer to what was actually happening in the world.

We Can Do Things Better, But What Should We Do Differently?

To me, this is the big question. I'm not saying schools are like businesses, because they are not. I'm also definitely not saying students are like consumers, because they are not.

Instead, let's take this lesson and apply it to our schools, with a focus on change. We know the world around us is constantly changing and many of those changes are affecting the everyday lives of our students and teachers:

- ◆ Work has changed, is changing, and will change (read this Whitepaper[1] by BrightBytes for some great information).
- ◆ Post-secondary education (and opportunities)[2] has changed, is changing, and will change.[3]
- ◆ Our learners are different and they learn differently (their brains work differently, awesome article from *Wired*).[4]

- Video Killed the Direct Instruction Star . . . (if there are complete courses of college professors teaching chemistry . . . what can our teachers do that they can't?).
- If Google Can Answer Every Question[5] . . . what is a valid assessment? (Hint: it can't answer every question).
- The classrooms walls are being ripped down[6] whether we like it or not (I tend to like it!).
- The world is flat[7] . . . which means more people have opportunities that didn't exist before.

So, if all this change is happening, and we know that change is going to be a "constant" in our lives . . . let's come together to see what needs to be done differently.

Here are some questions I'm asking, as a school leader, right now—and they are questions that need to be asked continually over time:

- How can we shape our learning activities and assessments to match what the world actually looks like right now?
- How can we create a curriculum cycle that is flexible and adaptive enough to allow for doing things differently each year, if need be?
- How can we focus on student-centered learning opportunities all of the time, instead of some of the time?

Netflix isn't a perfect model to look at, but we can take a few things away from its story. It has changed along with the world, instead of fighting back at it. It has proactively modeled its business practice on the reality, instead of past practice.

We, too, need to take a proactive approach to our change in schools. Our actions matter. Our actions will have impact. Our actions will drive innovation. And those who fail to take action will fall behind, just like Blockbuster.

Attitude: What We Can Learn from Thomas Edison

According to a 1961 *Reader's Digest* article by Edison's son, Charles, Edison calmly walked over to him as Charles watched a fire destroy his dad's work in a plant fire. In a childlike voice, Edison told his 24-year-old son, "Go get your mother and all her friends. They'll never see a fire like this again." When Charles objected, Edison said, "It's all right. We've just got rid of a lot of rubbish." Later, at the scene of the blaze, Edison was quoted in *The New York Times*[8] as saying, "Although I am over 67 years old, I'll start all over again tomorrow." He told the reporter that he was exhausted from remaining at the scene until the chaos was under control, but he stuck to his word and immediately began rebuilding the next morning, without firing any of his employees.

Was there any other viable response? In the new book, *The Obstacle Is the Way: The Timeless Art of Turning Trials into Triumph*,[9] author Ryan Holiday says there wasn't. Sure, Edison could have wept, yelled in anger, or locked himself in his house in a state of depression. But instead, he put on a smile and told his son to enjoy the spectacle.

Edison figured out that he lost almost $23 million in today's dollars. Worse yet, many lab reports, records, and prototypes were lost in the fire.

But after just three weeks, with a sizable loan from his friend Henry Ford, Edison got part of the plant up and running again. His employees worked double shifts and set to work producing more than ever. Edison and his team went on to make almost $10 million in revenue the following year.

Hearing that story blew me away. Thomas Edison had worked for years and years building this plant up, developing products and patents, and documenting so much research and progress. And then, in the blink of an eye, it was all taken away.

I think about us as teachers and leaders in education. We've spent so much time teaching, learning, and reaching students. We've spent years reforming schools, implementing initiative after initiative, and developing best practices.

But then everything changes. The world changes. Like Netflix and Blockbuster, we have a choice to make. We can either take action, or continue doing things the same way.

There's a great quote (Figure 3.2) that talks about *the problem of cognitive dissonance*. I have to do a gut check when I'm presented with information

Figure 3.2

Knowledge of Today

"Sometimes people hold a
core belief that is very strong.
When they are presented with evidence
that works against that belief,
the new evidence cannot be accepted.
It would create a feeling that is extremely
uncomfortable, called cognitive dissonance.
And because it is so important to protect
the core belief, they will rationalize,
ignore and even deny anything
that doesn't fit in with the core belief."

–Frantz Fanon

Figure 3.3

> "You never change things
> by fighting the existing reality.
> To change something, build
> a new model that makes the
> existing model obsolete."
>
> –Buckminster Fuller

that goes against what I currently believe. I have to ask myself whether I am open to new ideas, or simply fighting for the world to stay the way I like it.

Things are going to happen that we will not expect. The world will change in ways we cannot plan for, and we will not only have to deal with it, we will have to be role models for our children and students in *how* we deal with it, and *what* we do when it happens.

Building a New Model Together

Let's stop fighting change. Instead, let's build on the best practices we've developed over centuries as learners, and embrace next practices that reflect our world.

Let's stop fighting the tests. Instead, let's build new measures that show student achievement at a much higher level that any test could demonstrate.

Let's stop fighting each other on what platform or company is best. Instead, let's build resources and tools that work across any and all platforms, in order to give all teachers a chance to work with another inspiring educator.

Let's stop talking about what we can do to shape the future of education. **Instead, let's build it and inspire a generation of innovators.**

How We Can Inspire a Generation of Innovators

1. Be Expert Learners

I put this first on the list because we have to be master learners. We have to understand the science behind learning and the four stages to learning anything: attention, encoding, storage, and retrieval. This *first principle* building block of learning allows us to help students to be prepared for anything. In Liz Wiseman's award-winning book, *Rookie Smarts: Why Learning Beats Knowing in the New Game of Work,* she writes:

In a rapidly changing world, experience can be a curse. Careers stall, innovation stops, and strategies grow stale. Being new, naïve, and even clueless can be an asset. For today's knowledge workers, constant learning is more valuable than mastery.

We have to be expert learners, so our students can be expert learners. If we fail to grasp this shift, then we rely on being content experts when the content is already constantly changing.

2. Stay Informed or Get Left Behind

What are you feeding your brain? What are you reading? What videos are you watching? What YouTube channels do you subscribe to? What podcasts are you listening to?

How are you staying informed as a learner and leader? How are you staying updated as a parent and educator?

If you are not informed then you can only make decisions and plans for you and your students with outdated information. Here are some quick things you can do to stay informed:

◆ Get on Twitter. Follow these educators.[10] Browse the hashtags[11] and choose three that are relevant to what you do—or want to do. Follow the hashtags and join the chats if you can.

◆ Read the work of Peter Diamandis[12] and subscribe to his newsletter. You'll be informed on how things are changing in the world.

◆ Download the Flipboard App. Choose everything you are interested in to follow as a subject/topic. Check the app every day or every week to learn about those topics and read newly curated articles.

◆ When you find an article from Twitter or Flipboard that really speaks to you, sign up to follow that writer. Chance is they'll have more great stuff you'll like in the future.

3. Go Beyond Connection to Collaboration

Let's make things at conferences. Let's build products at Edcamps. Let's innovate when we connect instead of talking about what we *could do.*

The conversations are moving from Twitter and Facebook to Voxer and Google Hangouts. Teachers and leaders around the world are now creating projects together, starting movements together, researching together, and building products together.

Connection is great, don't get me wrong; but in order to inspire a generation of innovators, our students have to see us as creators and collaborators as well.

Find a problem (we all have many!). Find others that share that problem by connecting. Talk. Plan. Then build a solution together!

4. Forget About Labeling Learning

Differentiated. Blended. Personalized. Individualized. Flipped. Passion-based. Inquiry-based. Problem-based. Project-based.

On and on go the terms for learning. When really (as Bo Adams says), it's all about the *learning*. We can label learning, but it seems to be a futile exercise that excites only those that want to pretend like they are doing something new.

Do students have attention? Are they encoding the information in various ways? Are they storing it in their short-term, working, or long-term memory? Are they being given opportunities to recall that information and apply it?

That's learning.

A recent article by Howard-Jones in his paper for *Frontiers in Psychology*, points out that the concept of different learning styles is one of the greatest neuroscience myths:[13]

> *Perhaps the most popular and influential myth is that a student learns most effectively when they are taught in their preferred learning style.*
>
> *Learning styles do not work, yet the current research literature is full of papers which advocate their use. This undermines education as a research field and likely has a negative impact on students.*

The aforementioned evidence against learning styles is compelling. In 2004, Frank Coffield, professor of education at the University of London, led research into the 13 most popular models of learning styles and found there wasn't sufficient evidence[14] to cater teaching techniques to various learning styles. And a 2008 study by Harold Pashler,[15] psychology professor at UC San Diego, was scathing. Despite the preponderance of the learning styles concept "from kindergarten to graduate school", and a "thriving industry" devoted to such guidebooks for teachers, Pashler found there wasn't rigorous evidence for the concept.

Let's focus our attention on the actual learning, and not on labeling what type of learning our students are doing.

5. Focus on Building Great Relationships

In previous chapters we discussed how we learn, and why we learn. And beneath all the changes that we've seen, there is still something very human about learning: it is social and relationships matter. I believe innovative educator and author of *The Innovator's Mindset*, George Couros, sums it up perfectly:

> *We can no longer take the most human profession in the world and reduce it to letters and numbers.*

It doesn't work. We've tried it. Students need to be inspired by their teachers, challenged by their teachers and develop relationships with their teachers. Sir Ken Robinson puts it this way:

Figure 3.4

The Power of Teaching

I've said that education is a living process that can best be compared to agriculture. **Gardeners know that they don't make plants grow.** They don't attach the roots, glue the leaves, and paint the petals. **Plants grow themselves. The job of the gardeners is to create the best conditions for that to happen.** Good gardeners create those conditions, and poor ones don't. It's the same with teaching. **Good teaching create the conditions for learning,** and poor ones don't. Good teachers also know that they are not always in control of these conditions.

6. Don't Just Adopt Technology, Embrace It

If you think technology has reached the tipping point in how it's impacting learning, you are wrong. It's only just beginning. With the pace of change (especially in technology-related fields) ramping up, it's important to have a mindset that goes past adoption. Embracing technology means being a learner first, then figuring out how to use it with purpose.

When students see their teachers using technology with purpose, they want to use it with purpose. I see the work of students in Don Wettrick's Innovation Class and it's all about passion and purpose. Students are developing patents, creating sellable products, and launching movements; all with technology. Be that inspiration that your students need, by being a learner first and embracing the changes in technology.

7. Fight Weak Data with Better Measures

We all know that standardized test scores are not the best way to measure student success. But guess what, they are the easiest way. We also all know that what we measure matters. And the "measuring of achievement" is not going away any time soon.

Let's find better measures. If your standardized test scores are low but every student is graduating, going to college, a trade school, or getting a job once they leave, what does that say about your school? If students are getting rave reviews from internships, helping the community with programs, and impacting the global community with projects, what does that say about your school? If students are filing for new patents, inventing innovative procedures, and leading online movements, what does that say about your school?

Our kids cannot be reduced to numbers in a spreadsheet, or we'll inevitably be replaced by those that can "data dig" better than we can (hint: computers). But worse, when we use weak data to support and showcase what our schools are all about, we completely miss the most important piece of learning. Joe Bower said it the best:[16]

> Some things in life, however, are not made to be measured. While my height can be accurately described as 6'1" without debate, my personality, character, intelligence, athleticism and learning[17] can not be meaningfully reduced to a symbol. When we reduce something as magnificently messy as learning to a number, we always conceal far more than we ever reveal.
>
> The most important things that children learn in school are not easily measured. The most meaningful things in life may, in fact, be immeasurable. The good news, however, is that the most important and meaningful things that we want children to learn and do in school can always be observed and described. This is precisely why it is so important to remember that the root word for assessment is 'assidere' which literally means 'to sit beside'.[18] Assessment is not a spreadsheet—it's a conversation.

8. Empower Your Colleagues with Solutions

I was going to title this section: Replace Complaints (and Blaming) with Solutions. But it is more about empowering each other to find solutions, than it is to stop complaining and blaming. Here's the deal: we are all human. We are going to complain. It is very natural for us to blame others when things don't go the way we want them to go. Yet, none of that complaining and blaming matters. It doesn't help. It hurts.

I love how one of our elementary school principals this year made the focus for the year on "finding solutions". That's it. That's the mission. If there is an issue, or a problem, or a situation, let's be mindful enough to find a solution.

If we are going to inspire a generation of innovators, we are going to have to be problem-solvers ourselves. We are going to have to empower our colleagues to take action and have the right attitude. It's not going to magically happen. The greatest gift I ever received from a colleague is when I was complaining about my students' attitude towards my class. I had a "woe is me" attitude and couldn't believe they weren't engaged. When my friend (and peer) called me out, I had to think about solutions. That simple message led to the 20% Project in my class (more about this project in Chapter 5). It never would have happened if I didn't have empowering colleagues.

9. Take Your Classroom from a Space, to a Place, to a Home

I'll never forget one conversation I listened to as a new teacher. It was in a faculty meeting and one of our Art teachers stood up to talk about the *culture* at our building. There was a lot of complaining about student behavior, and a number of newly imposed rules for the hallways and classrooms. Yet, his words hushed the crowd and made us all think. He said, "If we want students to respect us and respect the school, we need to take this from a space, to a place, to a home for our students."

If your school and classrooms feel more like a space or a place for students, then what's the purpose of them learning in the classroom instead of in a cubicle in front of a computer? When our classrooms look like cemeteries, our students tend to follow suit. Lined rows of desks. Teacher up front. Students bored out of their minds.

And the best part is that 92% of teachers say they know the learning environment impacts student behavior and achievement, yet most feel like they are not in control of what it looks like and feels like. Let's change that this year, and make our places more like homes.

10. Allow For, Support, Make Time For, and Praise Creative Work

What we allow for in our schools and classrooms will ultimately open up avenues for new ideas to develop. If we don't allow for inquiry, choice, collaboration, digital tools, failure . . . then usually only the people in charge are allowed to have ideas.

Similarly, a constant complaint I hear from teachers and students is that they don't have enough time. It drives stress levels up, and brings innovative work to a halt when we create curricula and schedules that are jam-packed with content and pre-determined lessons. When we make time for reflection/self-assessment (look at Hattie's work), sharing, and making/tinkering, our students—and our teachers—actually go out and *try* new things.

Next is support. Take, for instance, a school that solely focuses on standardized assessments. The teachers are not supported by the administration by bringing in new ideas or curiosity to their profession. Then it is increasingly difficult for teachers to support students when they create or make. Often they'll never get the opportunity. Yet in schools like Wissahickon (where I taught), I was supported when I wanted to try something new in the classroom. Online and global opportunities like the Flat Classroom Project weren't looked down upon. And when my students wanted to try something outside of the box, or run with a project idea, I jumped at supporting their innovative work through ideas like Project: Global Inform. Support is a key ingredient to help those *new ideas actually work.*

When we change what we praise and look for in a classroom, students begin to adjust what matters. When we praise failure, look for resiliency, and assess the process (instead of only the final product) then students are empowered to share their work and grow as learners in a variety of ways.

Be Intentional About Innovation

Innovation starts with action. It starts with being intentional about how we lead, how we learn, and how we teach.

Notes

1 http://pages.brightbytes.net/rs/brightbytes/images/WP_21stCentury Workplace_FINAL.pdf.
2 www.theatlantic.com/features/archive/2014/08/the-future-of-college/375071.
3 www.huffingtonpost.com/dr-ricardo-azziz/a-looming-challenge-higher-education_b_4855108.html.
4 www.wired.com/2014/08/end-of-absence-how-technology-changes-our-brains-society-children.
5 http://edu.blogs.com/edublogs/2010/06/finding-questions-that-google-cant-answer.html.
6 www.theguardian.com/teacher-network/teacher-blog/2013/jun/19/technology-future-education-cloud-social-learning.
7 www.aasa.org/SchoolAdministratorArticle.aspx?id=5996.
8 http://query.nytimes.com/mem/archive-free/pdf?res=F40614FF3F5C13738DDDA90994DA415B848DF1D3.
9 Holiday, R. (2014) *The Obstable Is the Way: The Timeless Art of Turning Trails Into Triumph.* New York: Portfolio.
10 https://twitter.com/ajjuliani/lists/must-follow-for-upsd.
11 http://cybraryman.com/edhashtags.html.
12 http://diamandis.com.
13 http://qz.com/585143/the-concept-of-different-learning-styles-is-one-of-the-greatest-neuroscience-myths.
14 Cottrell, S. (2003) *Skills for Success: The Personal Development Handbook.* Basingstoke: Palgrave Macmillan (main library 331.702 COT and at St Luke's Library 378.170281COT).
15 www.psychologicalscience.org/journals/pspi/PSPI_9_3.pdf.
16 www.joebower.org/2015/12/assessment-and-measurement-are-not-same.html?m=1.
17 www.joebower.org/2012/04/one-average-to-rule-them-all.html.
18 www.joebower.org/2010/08/to-sit-beside.html.

Chapter Reflection

What ideas resonated with you from this chapter? Take notes, draw, brainstorm, and reflect in the space below. Share your ideas on Twitter using the hashtag #beintentional.

4

Why We Need Intentional Innovation

Innovation is a tricky word. We often use it to describe something new and shiny. Other times we use it to explain how certain people think. Mostly we throw it around without ever defining what it means. And that is the simplest way for any word to lose its power and meaning.

I tend to go with the definition by Geoff Mulgan:[1] **"new ideas that work"**.

It's short, but very clear. Innovation is one part "new ideas" and one part "working".

That does not mean it can't be based on something old (and reinvented), or that it can't have failures along the way. But when we truly innovate we've taken something new and made it work—regardless of how long the process was.

This definition also allows for both incremental and exponential innovation. That is to say, Elon Musk making a better electric car[2] (incremental) and creating a new mode of transportation called the Hyperloop[3] (exponential) can both be seen as innovative, when they work.

Why Innovation in Education Should Be Intentional

Now that we've roughly defined what innovation is, we need to look at the word "intentional" and how it impacts innovative work.

I've been a student, teacher, parent, and now administrator in K-12 schools. I've worked with college institutions, consulted for large organizations, volunteered for non-profits, and spoken to companies; all of which were looking to innovate in education.

It seems that every place I go, *people are looking to innovate.*

The challenge is *how* to innovate, and do so with purpose, in order to have an impact on your organizational, institutional, or educational goals.

I was talking recently to a former student of mine who just returned from a semester abroad. He was explaining how much he learned in the past couple of months and how his view on the world continued to change as he met new people. He brought up the Flat Classroom Project[4] we did in 10th grade. He said:

> *I thought that project was a lot of work at the time. I also remember think-ing how much work I was doing and that some of my global peers weren't doing work they were supposed to be doing. Then you told us that it was easy to stay on top of your work when you had a computer at school and at home internet access wherever you went, and a schedule set up that made it all possible . . . This trip made me start to think about my life in those terms again. It made me realize that privilege impacts so much more than how people treat you. It impacts what you can do in life a lot of the time.*

Wow. These were profound words about privilege through a global perspec-tive. It made me go back and think about the purpose of taking my students through the Flat Classroom Project.

The project was innovative, especially for its time, because it was a global collaborative project, where students worked and learned with each other to develop a rationale for how the world is changing, and then make videos to explore what this means for all of us.

It was a new idea that worked, thanks in large part to Vicki Davis and Julie Lindsay who created it.

However, in choosing this project, I was very intentional as a teacher. I'm sure Vicki and Julie were just as intentional when they created what the project would look like.

My 10th grade English course was focused on multi-cultural and global perspectives on literature. Our essential question was, "How do I inhabit and embrace the global community?" This project tied together many differ-ent pieces of our work all year long:

◆ How assimilation impacts cultures and society;
◆ How technology has worked to eliminate ethnocentric perspectives;
◆ How the flattened world will shape our future; and
◆ How literature reflects/mirrors society.

Therefore, this innovative project was perfect for my students because it would expand their understanding of our "big ideas" from the course, put them in real global collaborative situations, use technology for a purpose, and support their understanding of cultures and how we can work together to solve big problems.

Previously, I had done a number of projects with my students that I considered innovative (in that they were new ideas that worked), but none of them had the targeted impact on my students' learning in the same way as the Flat Classroom Project.

The key was intentional innovation.

To be intentional is to have a purpose and goal for what you are going to do. And intentional innovation is so powerful because we are innovating for a reason that is both meaningful and relevant to the cause/work.

What Risks Will You Take This Year?

I've seen more and more administrators and school leaders *urging* their teachers to take risks in their classroom this year.[5] I've heard from teachers what risks they are going to urge their students to take this year in their learning.

As teachers and leaders, *we are the guides* that help our students navigate these risks. We help them become heroes of their own story, by allowing for inquiry and choice in the classroom. And heroes don't sit around all day; they are actively taking risks.

Guide on the side (a term we throw around) is *actually a guide*! Someone who does more than hand over a map. A guide is someone like Yoda, Haymitch, Gandalf . . . who actively participates in helping the hero of the story (our students) to find success and navigate failure.

As guides, we can support our risk takers (the heroes of the story) in a variety of ways:

◆ We are expert learners.
◆ We can help students reach out to mentors.
◆ We can build learning communities that share failures and success.
◆ We can create a culture of learning that goes above and beyond what any test can measure.

But, please be intentional. Be intentional in the innovative work you do in schools, with students, and in any organization or institution. Be intentional with what path you set students on, and what paths they choose for themselves.

Just as we must use technology for a purpose for it to be successful, we must innovate in ways that are meaningful and relevant for it to have an impact.

Who Gets to Decide What Is Innovative?

I was talking with a teacher in my school district who said, "I just don't know if we should try this again in class. It seems like lots of people online have already done it, and I read a few blog posts that really criticized it."

I asked her, "Well, how did it work for you and your students the first time?"

"It was great," she said. "The kids enjoyed it and want to do it again. But a lot of people think it's all fun and games, not necessarily any substance to it."

I asked again, "Well, what do you think? Did it have substance and purpose in your class?"

"Yes, the kids were engaged and excited to learn. It was fun but also had purpose."

I left the conversation happy we had talked it out, but also upset that others who were not in her class were trying to dissuade her from trying something new (and in her mind innovative) with her students. In fact, I was a bit angry.

I've seen a lot of blog posts, articles, and videos where people are deciding what's innovative for everyone. And while I respect the opinions of everyone sharing their thoughts online, I'm a bit tired of the judgment being placed on teachers, school leaders, and other people trying to do innovative work.

There seems to be a big misconception that if something was done before and it didn't work in one classroom, then it's not innovative. Or if something has been done for five years already and it's being done "everywhere" then it's not innovative.

If you're a teacher, school leader, or parent who is trying something new to help your kids and your students learn better, that's awesome! Don't let anyone tell you that it's not innovative, that you shouldn't try it, and that it's already been done before.

We seem to forget that we are all on this giant continuum. Some of us jump on at different points, some of us experiment with different things, and some of us don't know everything that's been done before in other schools.

It's About the People Doing the Work

If you're a teacher and want to flip your classroom and you think that's going to work for your students, then do it—don't let anyone tell you otherwise.

If you're thinking of doing Genius Hour or a 20% project but you're seeing people online say, "well that's not enough", just do it. What your students are learning and creating will prove them wrong.

If you want to use a new app, new tool, or something that people are saying is just another "fad", go ahead and experiment. If you think it's going to work in your classroom, with your students (that you know best), then go and do it, and don't let others tell you it's not innovative.

If you want to use pencil and paper (or cardboard and duct tape) in new ways then go and do it because that's what's innovative and may work for your situation.

There's not some governing board that gets to decide what's innovative and what's not. There's not some expert out there that gets to say, "well that won't work in your classroom" because they don't know your classroom. They don't know your kids. They don't know your circumstances.

I wish we would spend less time debating what's innovative work, and more time celebrating what's happening in our schools right now, this very moment.

Because there is so much good happening.

Don't let others sway you from trying something new in your class or school. Don't let the opinions of people who *supposedly* know better stop you from doing things that might work.

If it's a new idea to you and your students and it works in your class, then it's innovative.

The only people who get to decide what's innovative are the people who are actually doing the work: those that are teaching, leading, creating, sharing, and learning.

This book is about unleashing the belief that we can all innovate. We can all create. We can all make something new that works. It starts with us in the trenches doing the work every day.

Let's never forget that.

Notes

1 http://youngfoundation.org/wp-content/uploads/2013/04/Social-Silicon-Valleys-March-2006.pdf.
2 http://tesla.com.
3 www.spacex.com/hyperloop.
4 https://en.wikipedia.org/wiki/Flat_Classroom_Project.
5 http://ajjuliani.com/10-risks-every-teacher-take-class.

Chapter Reflection

What ideas resonated with you from this chapter? Take notes, draw, brainstorm, and reflect in the space below. Share your ideas on Twitter using the hashtag #beintentional.

Part 2
A Framework for Innovation

5

PLASMA: A Framework for Intentional Innovation

I know, I know, you're saying, "A.J., why do we need another framework in education?! And why, oh why, would you create another acronym that I have to remember?!"

I hope, if you've read this far, that you'll give me a chance to explain why I feel this framework is needed right now, and why I could care less about the acronym piece (PLASMA is kind of cool though, right?). Better yet, I hope you'll see the process and story behind PLASMA and how it has impacted my own work in the classroom and as a school leader—and, quite frankly, as a parent.

Let's Start at the Beginning

I'm an idea guy; that is, I have a lot of ideas. As a teacher I would constantly improvise, come up with new projects, lesson ideas, tweaks to traditional assessments, and have an organic approach to learning in my classroom.

But they were still my ideas.

I was failing to value, foster, and spark ideas from my students. In fact, I would sometimes hurt their creativity and flow by moving on too quickly.

Sir Ken Robinson says:

The role of the creative leader is not to have all the ideas; it's to create a culture where everyone can have ideas and feel that they're valued.

That was problem #1.

Problem #2 happened when I really began to reflect on what work my students were creating, making, and producing. Quite honestly, as a 1:1 classroom teacher (all of my students had devices), I had students who created more "digital fridge art" than anything else.

I was using technology to spice things up and engage my students, failing to realize that technology can be another form of extrinsic motivation. The same can be said for Project-Based Learning and all types of "learning" that we package as a *new way* for students to achieve. There was no autonomy, purpose, or levels of mastery given to my students; it was still the carrot and the stick, but in techno-form.

The issue is that it's still learning. No matter what we call it. And for learning to truly be innovative and inspire innovative work, it needs to be intrinsically motivated and extrinsically supported.

My teaching world was turned upside down with the 20% Project. I've written about this project extensively,[1] but the basic idea was that I gave my students 20% of their class time to learn and create anything they were passionate about and interested in, and they had to document and present what they learned and made.

At first, I believed that the level of innovative work I saw in this project was directly correlated to students having choice. And this was a huge piece to the puzzle. *But it was not the only reason.*

As I spoke with teachers around the world who were doing Genius Hour, 20% Projects and Passion Projects I kept hearing similar stories: the students struggled; the process was hard; and the results were uplifting.

In Working with Students and Teachers There Seemed to Be Common Threads That Connected the Work

1. Students were allowed to do so much more in class than they previously had in other learning experiences.
2. Teachers made time for certain collaborative and reflective activities, that often fall through the cracks when we are trying to cover curriculum.
3. Teachers, student peers, and other members of the school community supported students in their learning through a variety of means.
4. Teachers, administrators, and peers praised certain actions and looked for unique types of creative work that are often hard to assess through traditional measures.

In researching and pulling all of this information together while writing my first book, *Inquiry and Innovation in the Classroom*,[2] I created an infographic as a starter framework for innovation in our schools.

While this framework provided some actionable ideas and tips for bringing innovation into our schools, it still lacked the practical structure and correlation to actual innovative work.

I began working to develop this idea with a number of colleagues, to go beyond being a "guiding" graphic, and instead being something we can use in our classrooms and schools to foster intentional innovation.

Building a Framework That Matters

If you are like me, then you've come across your fair share of educational frameworks; whether it is UBD[3] (Understanding by Design) for backwards curricular planning, SAMR[4] (Substitute, Augmentation, Modification, Redefinition) for technology integration, or TPACK[5] for combining technology, content knowledge, and pedagogical awareness. There are many, many frameworks. Yet as I researched the connection of these frameworks to innovative work, I was often taken down a rabbit hole with no clear end.

Derek Muller, of Veritasium,[6] has created an epic video, *This Will Revolutionize Education*, where he talks about the fallacy of technology's impact on teaching and learning. I've shared this video when I speak about technology because it makes the point that learning is still about what happens inside our head, and teaching is still about inspiring, challenging, and motivating each learner.

Technology ≠ Innovation in Education

The key to this understanding is that technology has played—and will play—an important role in many types of innovation. From how we travel (horses, cars, boats, planes) to how we communicate (radio, TV, computer, internet) to how we live (electricity, solar power, etc.).

Yet, there have been few technological innovations that were created specifically for education. The internet has played an enormous role in allowing anyone in the world to learn anything they want, at any time, providing they have a device and internet access. And although it is one of the greatest learning tools of all time . . . it was not developed for that purpose.

The technology devices we bring into schools now—laptops, iPads, and smartphones—were not developed for educational purposes.

And the list could go on. Even the software used in most schools was primarily developed for business before it was used for education (think the Microsoft Office Suite and even Google Apps).

Someone whose ideas on innovation in education I greatly admire, George Couros,[7] has said:

Often, the biggest barrier to innovation[8] is our own way of thinking.

This can go both ways. Our thinking hinders us to move forward and try to create "new ideas that work" but it also limits how we think about innovation.

If we believe innovation in our schools is always correlated with technology, then we look for a new technology that can be a game changer. However, if we realize that technology plays a role in innovation, but is not necessarily the "new idea", then we can use it with a purpose to make those "new ideas" actually work!

The Intentional Innovation Framework

The PLASMA Framework connects the actions and intentions of the leader/ teacher to the types of learning and creating that ultimately takes place.

The **PLA** in PLASMA stands for **Praise**, **Look For**, and **Assess**. There is famous saying that "What you measure is what matters"; and this is very true in the teaching and learning world.

If our schools are only successful based on standardized measures, then it is no coincidence that many focus their efforts on the performance of these measures. For our students, this tends to mean they believe handing work in on time, being compliant, and doing well on traditional assessments is what makes them a good student. It's why a third of my 11th graders during

Figure 5.1

Praise/Look For/Assess	→	Empowered to Share and Grow …
Support	→	Create and Make …
Make Time For	→	Try New Ideas/Ways …
Allow	→	Develop Ideas …

the 20% Project asked if they could just get a handout with a rubric instead of having to think for themselves what they wanted to learn. Yet, when we change what we praise and look for in a classroom, students begin to adjust what matters. When we praise failure, look for grit, and assess the process (instead of only the final product) then students are empowered to share their work and grow as learners in a variety of ways.

The **S** in PLASMA represents what we **Support**. Take for instance a school that solely focuses on standardized assessments: the teachers are not supported by the administration in bringing in new ideas or curiosity to their profession. So it is increasingly difficult for teachers to support students when they create or make. Often they'll never get the opportunity. Yet in schools like Wissahickon (where I taught) I was supported when I wanted to try something new in the classroom. Online and global opportunities like the Flat Classroom Project weren't looked down upon. And when my students wanted to try something outside of the box, or run with a project idea, I jumped at supporting their innovative work through ideas like Project: Global Inform. Support is a key ingredient to help those *new ideas* actually *work*.

The **M** in PLASMA represents what we **Make Time For**. A constant complaint I hear from teachers and students is that they don't have enough time. It drives stress levels up, and brings innovative work to a halt when we create curricula and schedules that are jam-packed with content and pre-determined lessons. When we make time for reflection/self-assessment (look at Hattie's work), sharing, and making/tinkering, our students (and our teachers) actually go out and *try* new things.

The **A** in PLASMA stands for **Allow**. What we allow for in our schools and classrooms will ultimately open up avenues for new ideas to develop. If we don't allow for inquiry, choice, collaboration, digital tools, and failure, then usually only the people in charge are allowed to have ideas.

Allowing goes beyond "letting students use devices" in the classroom. It is allowing for setbacks, for trials, for pilots, and for mistakes that truly makes a difference.

How to Use the PLASMA Framework

There are three main ways to use the PLASMA Framework. Although, I'm sure as a reader and educator you will be able to finalize this as to how it is used best for you!

1. As a Self-Audit and Assessment

As noted researcher and author John Hattie's work, and many other studies, point out, self-reflection/assessment is a powerful learning tool. Using the PLASMA Framework as a self-audit provides a way of analyzing what you are allowing, making time for, supporting, and praising as a teacher or leader.

Then the second step is to correlate to and impact what students are doing in your classroom, or teachers are doing in your school.

2. As a Planning Tool

As a fairly new school administrator I'm still learning what it means to be a leader. One thing that is incredibly difficult to do in my role is be both *supportive* and *directive*. However, as I think about my first few years teaching (and coaching) the same was true. When should I be supportive? When should I be directive? What balance works best for which students and players?

With the PLASMA Framework I'm looking for a cause and effect. So last year when we **Allowed** our teachers to have full admin rights and control over their devices, I wanted to see the impact. We planned for certain measures and what would happen when we **Allowed** for admin rights.

How would we **Support** teachers in this process? What would we **Look For** as we moved forward? If all we did was **Look For** times when they abused this privilege and **Support** them when malware or a virus was detected . . . then really, would it have any type of impact on the work they were doing with students? Instead we can use PLASMA as a planning tool to continually refine how our actions as teachers and leaders lead to an impact in the classroom.

3. As an Observation Tool

Have you ever observed someone using the HEAT/LOTI[9] Framework or ISTE's iCot tool?[10] The tools themselves are not bad. After using them as observation tools I can understand why Scott McLeod helped build TRUDACOT[11] because it goes into more depth while giving more flexibility and accounting for levels of instructional impact.

PLASMA serves as a basis to objectively record what teachers are **Praising, Looking For, Assessing, Supporting, Making Time For**, and **Allowing**.

Pairing this observation with one that objectively records what students are doing in class can connect the actual actions and learning environment to what students do. This also can be used as a group work observation or team observation as well.

Notes

1   http://ajjuliani.com/20-time-guide.
2   http://ajjuliani.com/books/inquiry-innovation-classroom.
3   www.authenticeducation.org/ubd/ubd.lasso.
4   www.schrockguide.net/samr.html.
5   www.tpack.org.
6   www.youtube.com/watch?v=GEmuEWjHr5c.
7   www.gcouros.ca.
8   www.georgecouros.ca/blog/archives/5259.
9   www.loticonnection.com/our-frameworks.
10 www.pps.k12.or.us/files/information-technology/Technology_Checklist.pdf.
11 http://dangerouslyirrelevant.org/resources/trudacot.

Chapter Reflection

What ideas resonated with you from this chapter? Take notes, draw, brainstorm, and reflect in the space below. Share your ideas on Twitter using the hashtag #beintentional.

6

What to Praise, Look For, and Assess

Raise your hand if you have spent over 14,000 hours in school during your lifetime.

If you grew up in the Unites States, or a country with a similar education philosophy, chances are you spent 6.64 hours per day in school, 180 days a year, for 12–13 years.

Figure 6.1

Figure 6.2

That's a lot of slices.

840,000 Minutes

No matter how you slice it, that's over 14,000 hours—or 840,000 minutes.

The 6.64 average hours a day in school is actually better represented in minutes: 400 minutes per day, give or take a minute or two.

That's how much time each of our students (and each of us when we were students) spend in their K-12 journey: 400 minutes, or 180 days a year, so 2,340 days in total.

So, what are we actually doing with those 400 minutes each day?

Or a better question: **what are our students doing in those 400 minutes a day?**

The Quantitative Classroom

If you are a parent you may wonder every now and then what your kids are doing all day in school. But, as an educator, teacher, and administrator (oh yeah, and I'm a parent), I've wondered out loud what a typical day-in-the-life of our students looks like.

Figure 6.3

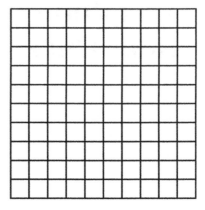

In an effort to make this as visually appropriate as possible, I'm sharing with you the *100 block theory of learning*.

The chart is shown in Figure 6.3 (hint: it's 100 blocks).

Each of those 100 blocks represents 4 minutes of time spent in school. So, when I was teaching HS English, each of my class periods would be 10 blocks (it was a 40-minute period). When I was an administrator at Upper Perk, our HS was on a block schedule at 80-minute periods (which would be 20 blocks).

It'll look different depending on what you teach, your schedule, and your school. But the 100 blocks are universal enough to work in all different settings.

Take, for instance, the national problem with sitting too much. It starts in school. American students will spend an average of 4.5 hours a day sitting.

Figure 6.4

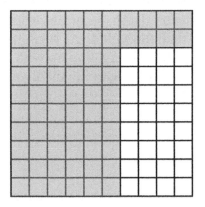

Almost two-thirds of our students' days are spent with them sitting in a seat; often listening to someone else talk, or being compliant in complete silence.

My daughter is 7 and my son is 5. I rarely see them sit at home for a full meal at the table, let alone for 270 minutes. When Sir Ken Robinson said, "schools kill creativity", it's tough to argue with him looking at stats like that. But I think he said it better here:

Many highly talented, brilliant, creative people think they're not—because the thing they were good at wasn't valued at school, or was actually stigmatized.

When we start to quantify how students are spending their 100 blocks of time in school, things start to look a bit different. I wonder if we even know much time we are potentially wasting.

The 100 Block Theory of Learning

Let me be very clear here; I'm not a scientist, nor do I play one on TV. But, according to the general definition of "theory", I'm going to take a chance and put something out to the world.

Definition: A theory is a statement of what causes what, and why, and under what circumstances. A theory can be a contingent statement or a proven statement. That is all.

My theory comes from observation as a student, as a teacher, as an administrator, and now as someone who gets to talk to teachers and administrators around the country and world about teaching and learning.

The theory itself is quite simple but, like anything, the follow-up is crucial.

Take, for instance, Albert Bandura's *social-cognitive learning theory*. Bandura noted that our behavior is changed when we see a person take a specific action and be rewarded for that action. In the future, we are more likely to take that same action. This is vicarious learning, in which we learn through imitation rather than through direct reinforcement.

Bandura then followed this observation up with studies and research to support (or refute) social-cognitive learning theory.

The observation created theory is then supported to change based on research and studies conducted.

How the 100 Block Theory Works

What we spend our time *doing* in school, will have a direct impact on the *learning* that takes place.

We will *do more* of what we *praise* as colleagues and leaders.

I know, I know. Ground breaking stuff here. But, honestly, what are we spending our time doing in school these days? And, how does it measure up to the learning that we are seeing?

For example, I'll take two areas of focus for schools that President Obama and First Lady Michele Obama had in their eight years in office.

First Priority: Let's Move

The physical and emotional health of an entire generation and the economic health and security of our nation is at stake.

—First Lady Michelle Obama at the *Let's Move!*
launch on February 9, 2010

The problem: Over the past three decades, childhood obesity rates in America have tripled, and today nearly one in three children in America are overweight or obese.

The focus: As the national initiative to ensure that 60 minutes of physical activity a day is the norm in K-12 schools across the country, *Let's Move!* Active Schools[1] equips schools with the resources and tools to increase physical education and physical activity opportunities for students.

Let's go back to the blocks to check this out:

Figure 6.5

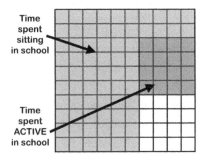

I love the effort to spend more time being physically active in school. But, if we want our kids to be healthy and active, we have to look at what we are actually doing in school. And most of what we are doing is sitting . . .

Even two 30-minute recesses can solve that problem entirely.

Another potential solution: What if we took all—or most—of those minutes in Figure 6.5 and turned them into standing, instead of sitting, minutes? Schools around the country have begun to embrace, and buy, standing desks for students. The research supports standing desks, and their impact on health, in many ways.

What the Research Says[2]

"Research by a number of experts supports this fidget-friendly mindset. A 2008 study found that children actually need to move to focus during a complicated mental task. The children in the study—especially those with attention-deficit/hyperactivity disorder (ADHD)—fidgeted more when a task required them to store and process information, rather than just hold it. This is why students are often restless while doing math or reading, but not while watching a movie, explained Dr. Mark Rapport, the supervisor of the study and professor of psychology at the University of Central Florida in Orlando.

Increasing students' activity level in the classroom provides physical benefits, as well. Dr. Donald Dengel, director of the Laboratory of Integrative Human Physiology and an associate professor at the University of Minnesota, co-authored a 2011 study that examined changes in caloric expenditure due to standing desks. His study found that participants using the desks burned 114 more kilocalories per day; or about half a candy bar. Dengel says:

> *That doesn't sound like a lot, but if you add that up for five days a week, it's about two-and-a-half candy bars per week, and over the course of the school year, it adds up to almost six pounds.*

Second Priority: STEM Education

> *We don't want to just increase the number of American students in STEM. We want to make sure everybody is involved. We want to increase the diversity of STEM programs, as well. And that's been a theme of this science fair. We get the most out of all our nation's talent—and that means reaching out to boys and girls, men and women of all races and all backgrounds. Science is for all of us. And we want our classrooms and labs and workplaces and media to reflect that.*
>
> —President Barrack Obama, March 2015

The problem: Despite our historical record of achievement, the United States now lags behind other nations in STEM education at the elementary and secondary levels. International comparisons of our students' performance in science and mathematics consistently place the United States in the middle of the pack, or lower.

Survey data from the National Center for Education Statistics show that teachers in grades 1–4 in self-contained classrooms reported spending an average of 2.3 hours per week on science instruction. Class time spent on science dropped from a national average of 3.0 hours per week in 1993–94, to 2.6 hours in 2000, and 2.3 hours in 2004 and 2008. Then there is the international data:

> *In 2015 on average across OECD countries, maths counted for 45 minutes of instruction time per day in primary education, and natural science for another 20 minutes. In relative terms, this translates to 17% of time devoted to maths and 8% devoted to science.*[3]

The solution: President Obama took a great number of steps to boost the amount of STEM teachers nationwide, funding towards STEM areas in school, and the Educate to Innovate[4] program is pushing STEM across the country in a wide variety of initiatives.

Figure 6.6

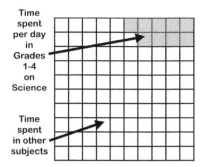

What do the blocks show us?

There has to be better (and more recent) data on the current time spent on STEM subjects in the classroom, but this is disheartening when there has been a national effort and yet our blocks show us that we aren't spending that much more time in school on these areas.

From the White House website:

> To date, this nation-wide effort has garnered over $700 million in public-private partnerships and hit major milestones in the following priority areas:
>
> 1. Building a CEO-led coalition to leverage the unique capacities of the private sector.
> 2. Preparing 100,000 new and effective STEM teachers over the next decade.
> 3. Showcasing and bolstering federal investment in STEM.
> 4. Broadening participation to inspire a more diverse STEM talent pool.[5]

The funding and commitment are there, yet we aren't seeing results where it really matters; which is what students are DOING in their time at school.

Another potential solution: What if we took all those millions of dollars to train current classroom teachers? Let's equip them with materials, resources, and professional learning opportunities that support STEM and make it possible to spend more time in school letting students do the work.

The 100 blocks don't lie.

You can do this type of 100 block analysis with your own classroom, your own students, or your own school. It works for all different roles in K-12 education.

It's about quantifying what we do, to see if our actions are helping or hurting our end goals for ourselves, our schools, and ultimately our students.

What administration spends time on will impact what our teachers spend time on, and what our students do in the classroom!

Figure 6.7

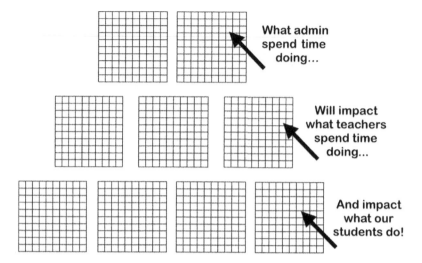

I had to answer this question myself as teacher six years ago. I looked at what I was doing, and realized I was trying to engage students with my content, my material, my resources, and my problems.

It wasn't until I gave them the choice in a Genius Hour and 20% Project that I saw what it meant to truly have an engaged and empowered class of students. That 20% of class time made all the difference in my students' school work, and in my life as a teacher.

Now, as a school administrator, when I praise and "shout-out" teachers for taking a risk and starting a Genius Hour, or inquiry-based project, or running a local watershed project, you better believe others are joining in.

Praising the outliers and risk-takers makes it that much easier for those on the fence to take a risk and fundamentally change what students are doing in school for those 400 minutes.

Breaking Out of the Pockets of Innovation

It seems that every school or organization I work with, speak at, or talk to has a similar problem to that shared above.

Pockets of innovation.[6]

In all honesty, the schools I've been a part of as a teacher, staff developer, and now administrator have dealt with this exact same issue.

Many of you are probably nodding in agreement right now. Maybe you've been in this situation. Maybe you've been one of the teachers or leaders in the pockets of innovation.

In fact, the pockets of innovation get a ton of praise and accolades from school leaders. They are often shared with the parents and community. The students in these pockets receive the benefit of having their work connected to an audience. The teachers in these pockets tend to get new opportunities for professional growth, which in turn pushes them to continually innovate in their classroom.

The pocket life is the good life.

Except it's a lot of work. It takes a lot of time as a teacher and school leader to keep the innovative and creative work going. It takes countless hours of reading, creating, collaborating, and facilitating to do this work.

And then, at the end of the school year, even after all the sharing, even after all the celebrating of this work, even after all the hours of professional development—we are often still left with pockets of innovation.

The cycle continues the following year. Many of the same teachers get new opportunities; many of the same students are celebrated for their work inside the pockets of innovation. It's great work. It's great learning. It should be shared!

But teachers, parents, school leaders, and community members are left wondering: what about the rest of the school?

The Explorers and the Settlers

There is a series of commercials for DirectTV, which have been on for some time now, about the "settlers" who would rather settle for what they currently have then try something new and better. It's easy for the settlers to point to their current way of living as a good life, and fight back against the new and innovative that is in the world.

Turns out there is a term for this: *loss aversion.*

In economics[7] and decision theory,[8] loss aversion refers to people's tendency to strongly prefer avoiding losses to acquiring gains. Most studies suggest that losses are twice as powerful, psychologically, as gains. Loss aversion was first demonstrated by Amos Tversky[9] and Daniel Kahneman.[10]

This leads to risk aversion,[11] when people evaluate an outcome comprising similar gains and losses; since people prefer avoiding losses to making gains.

We see this loss aversion happen in companies, organizations, and *schools.* I've actually heard of some school leaders sharing the video below at staff meetings to talk about whether or not they are promoting a culture of "settling" or a culture of exploring.

It's funny, but also concerning. Even those schools that have poked holes in their pockets of innovation and allowed it to spread far and wide may be left with pockets of settlers. Those that are risk averse and content to do things the way they've always done them.

You can tell I think a lot about this problem in schools. I wish I had a magic solution. But it seems in order to poke holes in your pockets of innovation and spread creative work beyond a few places, a lot of hard work has to take place.

In my time studying companies, researching, and talking to teachers and school leaders around the country (and the world for that matter), I've seen four areas that help spread this innovative type of work far and wide:

1. Sharing Is Not the Same As Highlighting What Works and Fails

There's a story about a woman at Google who lost the company millions. When she apologized to Larry Page, he told her, "I'm so glad you made this mistake. Because I want to run a company where we are moving too quickly and doing too much, not being too cautious and doing too little. If we don't have any of these mistakes, we're just not taking enough risk." (Read more at Reverse Engineering Google's Innovation Machine.[12]) Google is a company that actually values mistakes and is willing to pay for them. It's probably a nightmare for their accountants and risk-averse types.[13]

That story speaks volumes to anyone who works at Google, or anyone that wants to work at Google. Knowing that you'll be able to innovate and fail—and not be fired for it—makes the hard work less risk averse than at other companies.

I see many schools—mine included—sharing the stories of successes, and celebrating those who are in the pockets of innovation. But what about highlighting the initiatives, pilots, and projects that might not have been that successful? When we highlight what works and fails, we highlight the process and the work that goes into innovation, instead of only the final outcome. This helps build a culture where, as Sir Ken Robinson says, "Everyone's ideas are valued."

2. Reassurance of What Will Be Measured vs What Used to Be Measured

Tim Brown, CEO of IDEO (one of the most innovative companies in the world), offers this advice on building a culture of innovation:[14]

> What's important is an ability to create spaces where trust can happen, where risks can get taken. We tend in our operationally minded view of the world to try and mitigate and design out as much risk as we can, but if you want to innovate, you have to take risks. And to take risks you have to have some level of trust within the organization, because if people get penalized for failure, particularly the kind of failure that's most useful which is where you learn a lot, then they're not going to do it, in which case you're not going to get any innovation.

Many teachers I talk to say the same thing: "my school (or school leader) still cares about our scores on the standardized tests. How can I possibly prepare students for these high stakes tests, and also do creative work in my classroom?"

As leaders we have to own up to this. If we are consistently praising and measuring teacher and student success with measures of "accountability" then that is what we'll get . . . standard accountability.

Instead, when school leaders offer up new ways of measuring, praising, and assessing teachers based on creative and innovative pursuits/work, then that is what we'll get. What we measure will always matter, and we need to be intentional about shifting the narrative.

3. Empower Through Opportunities (Even for Those Struggling)

This one is simple. Give more people better opportunities for growth. Expand the pockets of innovation by supporting different teachers and having them attend conferences and Edcamps, give them online opportunities, and other avenues to empower their creative work.

The cycle of pockets of innovation will continue if the only people growing in a school are those that are already living in the pockets. We have to make the conscious decisions to spread the opportunities to all teachers and students.

4. A Framework for Creative Teaching and Learning

Tim Brown continued to speak about building a creative culture by saying:

> *Any organization that wants to innovate, wants to be prepared to innovate, I think, has to have a few things in place. One is—and perhaps the most important thing is—methods for having an open mind. A sense of inquiry, of curiosity is essential for innovation. And the quickest way for removing curiosity in my opinion is to have organizations that are too inward-facing, that don't spend enough time out in the world.*

What are your methods? How are you supporting inquiring and curious minds in your school or organization?

We often hear this myth of creative and innovative work; the myth that says they have to be "lightbulb" moments where one person has an amazing idea to share with the world. The truth is that all creativity doesn't work like that. It can be structured. It can be collaborative. There can be a framework and methods in place for creative work.

As we work towards "poking holes in our pockets of innovation", we have to consider the alternative: if we don't expand this creative work, we leave ourselves open to being disrupted by outside forces that we will have no control or influence over. Let's move education forward by moving everyone forward. It's not easy work, but it is the right work to be doing.

Notes

1   www.letsmoveschools.org.
2   www.nea.org/tools/47003.htm.
3   http://oecdeducationtoday.blogspot.com/2016/02/how-much-time-is-spent-on-maths-and.html.
4   https://obamawhitehouse.archives.gov/issues/education/k-12/educate-innovate.
5   https://obamawhitehouse.archives.gov/issues/education/k-12/educate-innovate.
6   http://ajjuliani.com/who-gets-to-decide-whats-innovative-in-education.
7   https://en.wikipedia.org/wiki/Economics.
8   https://en.wikipedia.org/wiki/Decision_theory.
9   https://en.wikipedia.org/wiki/Amos_Tversky.
10 https://en.wikipedia.org/wiki/Daniel_Kahneman.
11 https://en.wikipedia.org/wiki/Risk_aversion.
12 https://hbr.org/2008/04/reverse-engineering-googles-innovation-machine.
13 www.quora.com/Why-is-Yahoo-not-as-innovative-as-Google.
14 http://insights.som.yale.edu/insights/how-do-you-build-culture-innovation.

Chapter Reflection

What ideas resonated with you from this chapter? Take notes, draw, brainstorm, and reflect in the space below. Share your ideas on Twitter using the hashtag #beintentional.

7

Looking For and Assessing Real World Skills

We are now deep into the 21st century.

Communication is changing fast: my 7-year-old daughter and I just exchanged Snaps while in different time zones—I am in Chicago and she is outside of Philadelphia—with real-time interaction.

Collaboration has evolved to a point of instantaneous feedback loops. My colleague and I are on a shared Google Slides presentation changing and adding to slides for this week's presentation in real-time, able to modify and go back to old versions if need be. We also shared this with someone who is going to be in the presentation to get their feedback on a teacher perspective.

Critical thinking has become a necessity in order to not only solve big problems, but everyday issues; we know teachers learn best from other teachers, but it is increasingly harder to get teachers into each other's rooms due to sub shortages and other factors. One week we bought a 360 camera to film an elementary teacher's lessons to share with other staff, who watched using VR headsets to see the entire room as if they were in the classroom on a visit.

Creativity is a part of our everyday lives. No longer reserved for the few, we must all be creative and innovative to do our daily work. With all the great work currently happening in my school district, I'm working with a small team to create an innovative and simple way to share out the stories of teaching and learning with our community!

Yes, those bolded terms are what we commonly refer to as "21st century skills"; yet I'm fairly certain that these were always *needed* skills.

Socrates was talking about these 21st century skills over 20 centuries ago.

The Socratic Method is a form of cooperative argumentative dialogue between individuals, based on asking and answering questions to stimulate critical thinking[1] and to draw out ideas and underlying presumptions.

We still use this method today, and it is still effective.

Regardless of what we call them, the 21st century skills represent a type of skill that is not traditionally connected to standards and skills our students are evaluated on. Even though we know these types of skills are imperative to success in the workplace, in relationships, and in life, they are often still seen as "nice to have" instead of "need to have" for our students.

Seth Godin recently wrote an article, *Let's Stop Calling Them Soft Skills*,[2] in which he describes five categories of skills that we all look for in colleagues, employees, and students—yet we don't seem to value over other content and standardized skills.

What I love about Seth's view is that it is one from outside of education. He has created businesses, written books, designed products, and even started his own altMBA school. Seth believes these so-called "soft skills" are more important now than ever before.

Information is easier to access, share, and create. Communication, collaboration, critical thinking, and creativity are happening across many domains. Godin's five categories break it down into areas we can look to foster and empower in our schools:

The Five Categories of Real World Skills

Self-control: Once you've decided that something is important, are you able to persist in doing it, without letting distractions or bad habits get in the way? *Doing things for the long run that you might not feel like doing in the short run.*

- Adaptability to changing requirements
- Agility in the face of unexpected obstacles
- Alacrity and the ability to start and stop quickly
- Authenticity and consistent behavior
- Bouncing back from failure
- Coach-ability and the desire to coach others
- Collaborative mindset
- Compassion for those in need
- Competitiveness
- Conscientiousness in keeping promises

- ◆ Customer service passion
- ◆ Eagerness to learn from criticism
- ◆ Emotional intelligence
- ◆ Endurance for the long haul
- ◆ Enthusiasm for the work
- ◆ Ethics even when not under scrutiny
- ◆ Etiquette
- ◆ Flexibility
- ◆ Friendliness
- ◆ Honesty
- ◆ Living in balance
- ◆ Managing difficult conversations
- ◆ Motivated to take on new challenges
- ◆ Passionate
- ◆ Posture for forward motion
- ◆ Purpose
- ◆ Quick-wittedness
- ◆ Resilience
- ◆ Risk-taking
- ◆ Self-awareness
- ◆ Self-confidence
- ◆ Sense of humor
- ◆ Strategic thinking taking priority over short-term gamesmanship
- ◆ Stress management
- ◆ Tolerance of change and uncertainty

Productivity: Are you skilled with your instrument? Are you able to use your insights and your commitment to actually move things forward? *Getting non-vocational tasks done.*

- ◆ Attention to detail
- ◆ Crisis management skills
- ◆ Decision making with effectiveness
- ◆ Delegation for productivity
- ◆ Diligence and attention to detail
- ◆ Entrepreneurial thinking and guts
- ◆ Facilitation of discussion
- ◆ Goal setting skills
- ◆ Innovative problem-solving techniques
- ◆ Lateral thinking
- ◆ Lean techniques
- ◆ Listening skills

- Managing up
- Meeting hygiene
- Planning for projects
- Problem solving
- Research skills
- Technology savvy
- Time management
- Troubleshooting

Wisdom: Have you learned things that are difficult to glean from a textbook or a manual? *Experience is how we become adults.*

- Artistic sense and good taste
- Conflict resolution instincts
- Creativity in the face of challenges
- Critical thinking instead of mere compliance
- Dealing with difficult people
- Diplomacy in difficult situations
- Empathy for customers, co-workers, and vendors
- Intercultural competence
- Mentoring
- Social skills
- Supervising with confidence

Perception: Do you have the experience and the practice to see the world clearly? *Seeing things before others have to point them out.*

- Design thinking
- Fashion instinct
- Judging people and situations
- Map making
- Strategic thinking

Influence: Have you developed the skills needed to persuade others to take action? *Charisma is just one form of this skill.*

- Ability to deliver clear and useful criticism
- Assertiveness on behalf of ideas that matter
- Body language (reading and delivering)
- Charisma and the skill to influence others
- Clarity in language and vision
- Dispute resolution skills
- Giving feedback without ego

- ◆ Influence
- ◆ Inspiring to others
- ◆ Interpersonal skills
- ◆ Leadership
- ◆ Negotiation skills
- ◆ Networking
- ◆ Persuasive
- ◆ Presentation skills
- ◆ Public speaking
- ◆ Reframing
- ◆ Selling skills
- ◆ Storytelling
- ◆ Talent management
- ◆ Team building
- ◆ Writing for impact

The question then for us as educators (and as parents, etc.) is not only how we can work on building these skills, but more importantly how we can give students opportunities to learn, showcase, and *use these skills while they are in school*.

Bo Adams, the Chief Innovation Officer at Mount Vernon's Institute for Innovation, famously said:

> *If schools are meant to prepare students for the real world, then why doesn't school look more like the real world?*

These skills are important. They've always been important—maybe now more than ever before. In a world that is quickly changing, we need to continue to refocus our *why* on giving students the skills and knowledge to actively learn and pursue their interests, passions, and dreams.

The next time you are in a curriculum meeting, bring up these skills. The next time you create an assignment, think about how it ties into these skills. The next time you are at a faculty meeting or discussion with colleagues, ask whether or not these skills are being valued, looked for, assessed, and praised.

Giving Our Students the Chance to Develop Skills In the Wild

Mohini was a regal white tiger who lived for many years at the Washington DC National Zoo. For most of those years her home was in the old lion house—a typical 12-by-12-foot cage with iron bars and a cement floor. Mohini spent her days pacing restlessly back and forth in her cramped quarters. Eventually, biologists and staff worked together to create a natural habitat for her. Covering several acres, it had hills, trees, a pond, and a variety of vegetation. With excitement and anticipation, they released Mohini into her new and expansive environment.

But it was too late. The tiger immediately sought refuge in a corner of the compound, where she lived for the remainder of her life. Mohini paced and paced in that corner until an area 12-by-12 feet was worn bare of grass.

—Tara Brach on the Tim Ferris podcast

When I first heard the story about Mohini on a podcast, I immediately stopped and listened to it again. The analogy hit home.

We spend so much time preparing our students and slowly giving them choice and voice in their learning. We build up to the idea that when they finally leave our K-12 institutions they will be free and well prepared to take on the world and find their way in a new environment.

And yet, once you are given a choice, it's not easy to stop doing things the way you've been doing them your entire life. I've seen this first-hand as someone who almost failed out of college by my sophomore year (I had a 1.3 GPA). I changed my major six times, debating on "what I wanted to be" when I left school. It took me five years of college to find my way into teaching; mostly because I didn't spend any time scratching my itch in high school.

This is not to say that I didn't love my school experience. I did. Especially the extra-curricular and social aspects of school. But I rarely had the opportunity during school to navigate choices, create my own learning path, and break free from the game of school.

And this was not only my dilemma. I'm sure you faced similar challenges towards the end of your K-12 experience. All these existential questions start coming up like "Who do I want to be?" and "What do I want to do with my life?"

My students felt the same way at first when I presented them with choice in the 20% Project.[3] Other students find this to be the most difficult aspect of Genius Hour,[4] or other choice and inquiry-based learning[5] experiences.

When they have the choice to make their own learning path and create something they are interested in, many students feel trapped like Mohini the tiger.

My question (and it's not rhetorical) is, "Are we waiting too long to give our students choice and voice in their learning?"

When I see stories like Jason Seliskar's class having a student Edcamp,[6] I think about the potential bottled up in many of our students. When I watch videos of Caine's arcade and the global cardboard challenge[7] I get excited that the pendulum is swinging towards voice and choice at an earlier age. It's the reason I've been such a huge believer in the power of Genius Hour and 20% Projects to give our students the freedom to choose what they learn, what they make, and how they share it.

And yet I know how hard my 2nd grade daughter's teachers work to help her learn to read and write, understand basic mathematic principles, and guide her through the standards. I get the enormous pressures put on teachers to follow curriculum, prepare students to be successful on standardized assessments, and cover (instead of explore) specific content.

This is the reality of our situation.

So what can we do to make sure our students don't stay confined when given the opportunity to explore, make, and create on their own terms?

It's simple, really: make the most of every opportunity.

- That half day where you don't truly get anything accomplished? *Give students a Genius Hour.*
- That day before break where students have parties and often watch movies? *Let students make something.*
- That lesson you got through quicker than expected? *Challenge your students to solve a problem together.*

These are some of the examples I share when doing workshops and working with teachers, because I know they work and there are many teachers they can collaborate with that are already doing this type of learning.

I'm calling these ten examples "practical", because I believe they are doable. They work in most grade levels, in most schools, in most situations. However, as we have already talked about, you and your students are going to have to be the ultimate decision makers on whether or not any of these ideas would work.

1. Let Your Students Design the Learning

We all have those assignments, assessments, and units that need some revitalization. Often, we toil, thinking about how we can design a project or activity that is going to engage our students and empower them to do amazing work. One time, I didn't do this. One time, I asked and had a conversation with my students about the final assessment. And that one time turned into one of the most innovative projects I've ever been a part of— Project: Global Inform.[8] You see when I brought my students into the actual "designing" process, they took an enormous amount of ownership in how we would structure this final project, how we would grade this final project, and what the expectations were from them. Give your students a chance to design the learning with you and watch what can happen.

2. Run a Student-Led Edcamp

In 2014 I read about Jason Seliskar running[9] an "Elementary Unconference" as an Edcamp for his 4th grade students.[10] It was fantastic. These students created their own learning boards (just like in Edcamp), schedule for the day/class, and then become experts and learners in each other's session. Since then I've seen a number of schools and teachers run student-led Edcamps (here is one at a MS)[11] with great success. Why does it work? For the same reason Edcamp works for us teachers: students own the learning and the experience.

3. Collaborate Globally

I've written about this before. Participating in my first Global project (Flat Classroom Project) with my students changed me as a teacher, and my perspective of what types of learning experiences we can have "in school" with our students. Now there are many different global collaboration/learning experiences you can take part in. Whether it is joining up for the Global Read Aloud,[12] setting up a Mystery Skype call[13] with another class, or taking part in the first ever Global Day of Design,[14] your students can have the opportunity to work and learn with their peers from around the world.

4. Maker Projects and Design Thinking Challenges

Get your students making, creating, designing, building, and solving problems together with a Maker Project or Design Thinking Challenge. Check out the GlobalDayOfDesign.com[15] for free ideas and Maker Projects to get started.

5. Genius Hour and 20% Time

I get messages from teachers every day that have taken my free course on Genius Hour and 20% Time[16] or read my book, that are so excited about the work their students are doing. Genius Hour and 20% Time empower students to go into a depth around a topic that they are curious about. They learn, research, document, and share their process with the world. This eventually turns into a time to create (based on what they have learned) and then present with their peers and much larger authentic audience. Giving students choice to learn and create based on their interests is one of the best ways to create the conditions for innovative work.

6. Class Challenge (Do It Together!)

When I taught 11th grade English, one of the best experiences was collaborating with my good friend and colleague Steve Mogg on a daily basis. Throughout the year we taught a number of novels and stories that had mystery, court room scenes, and crime scene investigations. So, at the end of the year we created a Class Challenge project that would pit each of our classes against each other in a 3-day long "CSI: Wissahickon" challenge. At the start of the project we would present the crime that had taken place, who the key players were, and what students needed to solve. Each day we would leave a series of clues around our classrooms and the school that would help each class solve the crime. By the end of the 3 days they would have to present their case as a class and we would decide who had the winning argument. It was a blast, and incorporated all those problem-solving and team-building skills we were looking for—but the students always loved it because they worked together as an entire class to complete the challenge.

7. Community Project

I've recently witnessed students at my school building a beautiful table for the opening of a restaurant; working with the local watershed to solve water run-off problems; connecting with the community to run technology training; and putting on an entire TEDx production from start to finish. In each of these examples the project and work they were doing in school directly impacted the community. Sometimes we take for granted the opportunities for authentic learning experiences that are right outside our school doors. Connect with your local organizations, companies, and residents to see what types of projects would benefit the community, while also empowering students to solve problems and create solutions.

8. Teach the World What You Know (Create YouTube Tutorials)

I was in a 4th grade classroom last month, watching two Garnet Valley school district teachers explain circuits (and how they work). Afterwards, the students went through stations where they created circuits using Snapcircuits, Legos, and Minecraft! What was fascinating was how many of the students wanted to create Minecraft tutorial videos, teaching the world how to make and design circuits. The students took pictures of what they created and shared them via their teacher's class Twitter accounts. It reminded me that so many of our students want to teach the world what they know, and have the platform to do it (YouTube), but aren't always given the time in school. These teachers made time to allow their students to not only do the work, but share it with an audience!

9. Let Your Students Debate

My favorite day of the marking period as a teacher was the last day. Not because it was over, or grades were in, or we had a final assessment. It was the day I let my students argue and debate with me the entire class period. We created an Appeals Day where everything graded and assessed was up for discussion and debate. My students spent hours perfecting their arguments, teaming up with each other, collaborating, and building out their cases. It wasn't so much the fact that they could get points back (they could if their argument was strong) but instead it was the opportunity to debate. You can read more about Appeals Day later in this book (see pp. 108–111) or at "Why I Let My Students Argue for Their Grades".[17]

10. Write a Book/Release a Podcast Together

This last one is something I've seen in a number of schools, including our own. It's so easy now to publish a Kindle ebook or create a paperback book using CreateSpace and/or Blurb. Have a class writing assignment, then turn it into a published book by collaborating and putting it all together before getting in into the hands of parents, students, and other community members. The same thing can be done by recording students and creating a podcast that you can upload to the iTunes Podcast app using services like Libsyn or Stitcher.

Each of these ideas can be used and remixed in K-12 classrooms, but also with staff. If our teachers are still being assessed in traditional ways, it would be no surprise that they'll focus on traditional means.

What we look for and assess in each other is just as important as what we look for and assess in our students. In both cases the focus should be on authentic work that is relevant and meaningful to all involved.

Notes

1 https://en.wikipedia.org/wiki/Critical_thinking.
2 https://itsyourturnblog.com/lets-stop-calling-them-soft-skills-9cc27ec09ecb#.
   ym70tla6z.
3 http://ajjuliani.com/the-20-project-like-google-in-my-class.
4 http://ajjuliani.com/20-time-guide.
5 http://ajjuliani.com/research.
6 http://gettingsmart.com/2014/01/elementary-edcamp.
7 www.edutopia.org/blog/caines-arcade-cardboard-challenge-imagination-
   foundation-nirvan-mullick.
8 http://2030schools.com.
9 http://gettingsmart.com/2014/01/elementary-edcamp.
10 http://gettingsmart.com/2014/01/elementary-edcamp.
11 www.edcamp.org/blog-post/student-led-edcamp-period-glenn-robbins.
12 http://theglobalreadaloud.com.
13 http://blogs.skype.com/2013/09/16/introducing-mystery-skype-a-global-
   game-that-masks-learning-with-fun.
14 http://globaldayofdesign.com.
15 http://globaldayofdesign.com.
16 http://ajjuliani.com/20-time-guide.
17 http://ajjuliani.com/let-students-argue-grades.

Chapter Reflection

What ideas resonated with you from this chapter? Take notes, draw, brainstorm, and reflect in the space below. Share your ideas on Twitter using the hashtag #beintentional.

8

Supporting Relationships and Professional Growth

My grandmom is wise; and at 91 years old, she's still as curious as ever. One day we were having a discussion about the work we are doing in my school district right now, and my thoughts on where education and learning are going in the future.

The questions were fascinating, but even more so was the dialogue. She asked me whether or not I thought the increasing use of devices was taking away from face-to-face conversations, like the one we were having. We engaged in a back-and-forth on the "pros and cons" of having so much attention put on our phones and technology.

But this was not a one-sided debate where I was trying to convince her of the benefits of technology. My grandmom is still as active as ever, working in both the US and England throughout the year, while often traveling to Spain, and sometimes India, to do mission work. Medical issues have tried to slow her down over the years, but she keeps moving, talking, and traveling more than most of us do!

She has built an email list over the years (way before it was cool to build an email list) and regularly communicates with her friends, family, and those interested in the work she is doing. She has seen how technology has the power to connect people, but also realizes that it is often a "starting place" for relationships, or a "continuing" place for information.

Then she hit me with the quote that I was then thinking about all night:

It all comes back to relationships. Whether you use technology or have face-to-face conversations, it has to be about building that relationship if anything different is going to happen.

Boom. Drop the mic, grandmom!

Great Schools and Great Teachers Focus on Relationships

I've been lucky enough to be in some amazing schools and teacher classrooms over the past few years. Without fail, the #1 trait I see in each of these places is a focus on relationships. The relationships come from having opportunities for inquiry, challenging students, solving problems together, and doing work that is meaningful. But they also come from small side conversations, moments in the hallway, supporting outside of the classroom, and taking longer than expected to talk about an issue in class.

There has been a tremendous amount of pressure put on teachers and administrators to focus on everything else in education. The focus has been ramped up on data, differentiation, and individualized instruction.

Yet we can talk about all the data we want, but it won't make a difference if you don't have relationships with those teachers, and if those teachers don't have relationships with their students.

We can differentiate instruction all we want, but as the late great Rita Pierson[1] said:

A colleague said to me, 'They don't pay me to like the kids. They pay me to teach a lesson. I should teach it. They should learn it. Case closed.'

Well, I said to her, 'You know, kids don't learn from people they don't like.'

She said, 'That's a bunch of hooey.'

And I said to her, 'Well, your year is going to be long and arduous dear.'

It's not only for the kids that relationships matter; it's for all of us. Think of the best teachers you've had. Think of the best leaders you've worked for. Think of the best colleagues you've worked with.

In my case, they all put the focus on relationships first, and everything else second.

It's easy to get caught up in the "future of learning" and miss out on what has always worked when it comes to learning: relationships.

Yet nowadays, relationships can look very different. The human and social lens of learning has never been more important, but there has also never been more ways to build, sustain, and cultivate a relationship around learning.

Gary Vaynerchuck put this into perfect perspective when talking about relationships built with technology:

Figure 8.1

Are you using today's technology to build learning relationships? Are you meeting kids where they are? Are you meeting teachers where they are? Are you meeting parents where they are?

The future of learning is a lot like the past of learning, it centers around the human/social side of curiosity, creativity, and adaptation.

But the one thing that is very different, is how many avenues we have for reaching and growing the human/social side of learning. My grandmom said it right: **the focus on relationships should never change, even if the way to build those relationships does change.**

Why Teachers Learn Best from Other Teachers

Ahh, in service. Whether it is at the beginning of the school year, end of the school year, or smack dab in the middle of the school year . . . it seems like there is never a good time for school-wide in service.

Part of the problem I had with in service as a teacher is that it never seemed "worth my time" to sit and listen to someone from district administration talk, go through PowerPoint slides, and share out the new initiative our state was planning on doing to ramp up student achievement.

On the flip side, my cynicism usually melted away (almost immediately) when another teacher was presenting, sharing, or leading us during in service time. In fact, when I look back at my most valuable learning experiences as a teacher, they are almost always with colleagues and other teachers, instead of with an administrator, consultant, or presenter.

Flash forward a couple of years and now I'm in an administrative role, planning in services and realizing just how hard it is to plan an in service that is meaningful, relevant, and worthwhile to our teachers' time. Yet every time I've had teachers lead an in service or professional development session at my district, it seems to have a positive impact on everyone.

Teachers learn best from other teachers. This is not to say teachers don't learn a lot in a variety of other settings and situations, but from everything I've seen and experienced, it makes a lot of sense to have teachers leading professional development and training whenever possible.

Here are a few reasons teachers learn best from other teachers:

1. The Shared Hope

Anthony Gabriele and I taught HS English together for five years in the same school. Our conversations centered around the challenges our students faced, and the amazing work many of our students would do after being challenged and pushed—maybe a little more than they had wanted to be. In the midst of all the negativity that can sometimes float around a school, it was often these conversations with colleagues that raised me up and brought me back to the real reason we teach.

2. The Shared Struggle

I remember during one of our "Best Practices" in services where teachers could facilitate and choose which sessions they wanted to attend, I was speaking about the 20% Time project in my class. As I spoke about the lack of intrinsic motivation of my class, so many teachers resonated with this issue. Although my solution of giving 20% class time to work on a Passion Project seemed a bit radical, we all had the same shared struggle. It's hard to motivate students who aren't necessarily motivated by anything school can offer them (grades, rewards, etc.). This understanding brings teachers together and makes learning with each other meaningful and relevant.

3. A Deep Level of Respect

When colleagues at my current school district were sharing what they do with technology in their classrooms, there was a deep level of respect in the room. The presenters weren't an outsider (or district admin) sharing what "could" or "should" work in the classroom; they were teachers explaining how they did this work with the same students and same restrictions that each and every teacher who was sitting in that session faced, day in and day out. The level of respect for each other as colleagues in that room made the session impactful in ways that another presenter could never have managed.

4. Communal Experience and Language

The first session I ever led as a teacher during a district in service was (funny enough) on creating podcasts with your students. I was a second-year teacher, and a bit nervous to share this project and information with all of these teachers I looked up to in our school. But the session went so well because I could talk the same language and reference communal experiences that would happen to all of us. For example, I shared how one student truly read the book and knew the information, but froze up in front of the class. The podcast allowed all students to refine their message and have the class learn from them, regardless of their public speaking issues. Every teacher in that room had dealt with a similar situation, and our communal understanding made it easy to engage in deep learning that would matter in a classroom.

5. It's Fun to Learn with and from Colleagues

Steve Mogg is one of the best teachers I know. We coached and taught together for seven years. He's also hilarious. So when Steve ran a session on Twitter for teachers in our district, people signed up expecting to have a good time. And they did. But they also learned a lot along the way. Sometimes we take "professional development" too seriously and forget that learning can and should be fun, especially when it is with our colleagues. Teacher-led PD is one of the best ways to uplift a staff, and give them an awesome learning experience at the same time.

Supporting professional growth and relationships is not relegated to inside our schools any more. We know social media, blogs, and online communication has revolutionized the way we talk, work, and collaborate with each other. Yet it's often hard to see which pieces of this new social context are building relationships and learning. Our role as leaders is to support the growth and enable opportunities for more people to learn from others, whether inside our schools or online.

Innovation Needs People (Both Online and Offline)

It's been seven years since I joined Twitter. To be honest, I didn't know what Twitter was all about when I joined. I knew that I wanted to share what I was writing with the world, and besides my mom, my friends, and my wife (sometimes), there was no one out there who seemed particularly interested in what I was writing about: teaching and learning.

At the time, I didn't know many other people who were educators, and I sure didn't know many people who wanted to talk about education (much less transform education). There was almost no one in my school who was connected online with other teachers and leaders.

Seven years ago finding another teacher online to connect and collaborate with was like finding a flower in the middle of a desert. Today, finding teachers to connect and collaborate with feels more like finding a flower in the middle of a rainforest.

Technology—Twitter and blogging in large part—has transformed my thinking on education, my perspective on teaching and learning, and my view on how we can best empower our students.

But I didn't see this coming seven years ago.

I didn't see how technology could do all of this, because I wasn't able to see the people. Five years ago I was trying every new tech tool to come out. I was glogging with glogster. I was threading with voice thread. And I sure was writing and editing in real-time with Google Docs! But the technology was not transforming me; it was not transforming my classroom, because it was just technology.

As change continues to sweep education (much due to changes in technology) it is so important to remember the people.

Tech Can Be a Bridge, But People Make It Move (We Are Connectors)

Technology connects us to new tools, resources, and information. It also bridges the time and global gap between people. My first experience with global collaboration was during the Flat Classroom Project (started and led by Vicki Davis and Julie Lindsay). Students in my 10th grade English class were connecting with students from Qatar, Australia, England, Romania, and Canada. We were using Wikis, a Ning site, and other forms of technology to make connections and do work with students and teachers from around the world. However, my students and I will never remember how technology allowed us to bridge this time and distance gap. Instead we'll remember the connections; what it felt like to work with someone in a different time zone and country; and what the summit at the end of the project looked like compared to our normal class presentations!

With many amazing global collaborations going on like the Global Read Aloud,[2] and some awesome new global collaboration platforms, it's important to remember that technology may lay the bridge between people, but we still need to interact to make the learning move.

Tech Is a Drill, But People Have to Aim, Prep, and Finish (We Are Builders)

A few years ago I've been part of an amazing revitalization of our Industrial Arts program into a Maker department. We've built an xLab at Upper Perkiomen High School[3] and provided all kinds of tools like 3D Printers, a vinyl cutter, a heat press, and a CNC router to make the space allow for any type of building. But even with these awesome tools, our students have to do the work of building; our teachers have to do the work of making lessons, creating projects, and guiding during the design and making process. Without people using these tools, they wouldn't be transformational.

Tech Is a Mindset, But We Have to Be Willing to Change (We Are Growers)

Many of the people I meet through blogging, Twitter, and going to conferences have something in common: they aren't afraid of change. It seems that technology adoption in education lends itself to a type of person who understands the need for transformation at some level, and embraces the notion that things are going to be different.

To that extent, technology also helps us to give. It allows us to give new ideas to our colleagues, new experiences to our students, and make new connections that may transform our personal practice.

When I realized that people, not just technology, were the key to transforming teaching and learning . . . that's when the real fun started.

When we support our students, our colleagues, or our staff with real, tangible ways to connect and learn from each other, that's when innovation starts to flourish.

Notes

1 www.ted.com/talks/rita_pierson_every_kid_needs_a_champion?language=en.
2 http://globalreadaloud.com.
3 http://ajjuliani.com/beyond-makerspaces-why-we-created-an-xlab-at-our-school.

Chapter Reflection

What ideas resonated with you from this chapter? Take notes, draw, brainstorm, and reflect in the space below. Share your ideas on Twitter using the hashtag #beintentional.

9

Making Time for Creative Work

I distinctly remember learning how to type. It was hard. I had been a "hunt and peck" perfectionist up until the age of 14, when my school provided a computer course focused on the keyboard.

My teacher would shout out commands as we feverishly tried to get our fingers in the right place.

"ASDF!"

"JKL;!"

For a long time, I could still type faster by hunting and pecking. But as I continued to practice, my words-per-minute count grew, and I was able to type without looking at the keyboard.

By the end of that year, my hunting and pecking days were over. I had successfully assimilated to a QWERTY typist, and I've never looked back.

Interestingly, I never questioned the layout of QWERTY, or where it came from. I assumed (I tend to do that) that it was designed for speed and thought this was the best it could get.

Then I came across Nassim Nicholas Taleb's book, *Fooled by Randomness*. In one particular section, Taleb brings up the QWERTY keyboard, and the backward reason for how it was designed:

> *The arrangement of the letters on a typewriter is an example of the success of the least deserving method becoming successful. Our typewriters have the order of the letters on their keyboard arranged in a non-optimal manner.*

As a matter of fact, in such a non-optimal manner as to slow down the typing rather than making it easier to type faster.

This was done deliberately in order to avoid having the ribbons become jammed as they were designed for less electronic days of yore. Once we started to build better typewriters and computerized word processors, several attempts were made to change the keyboard in order to make them more efficient for typing purposes.

All of these attempts failed. People had been trained on "QWERTY" keyboards and their habits were too sticky for change. This is called a "path dependent outcome" and it has thwarted many attempts at modeling or changing behavior.

As Taleb points out, in 1874 when American inventor Christopher Latham Sholes[1] first designed the QWERTY layout, its purpose was to keep the keys from jamming; not for speed, accuracy, or efficiency of getting the words onto paper.

Regardless of how the world changed, the QWERTY keyboard never got an update, because it worked "well enough" and people did not want to change.

Designing for Function, Not Change

Sholes used the design thinking process to develop the typewriter,[2] first starting out by looking, listening, and learning about current issues with other typewriter designs:

Sholes had been for some years developing the typewriter, filing a patent application in October 1867. However, the original key layout, with the second half of the alphabet in order on the top row and the first half in order on the bottom row, led to some problems. The keys were mounted on metal arms, which would jam if the keys were pressed in too rapid succession.

Sholes then began to ask questions and understand the actual problem, before creating a prototype:

Sholes' solution was separating commonly used letter pairings, such as "ST", to avoid these jams, effectively allowing the typist to type faster, rather than slower.

Next was a focus on highlighting what was working, and fixing what was failing in his initial design. This iterative process brought about change that was again focused on solving the jamming problem:

He went through several design iterations, attempting to bring the type-writer to market. When he sold the design to Remington in 1873, the QWERTY layout looked like this:

2 3 4 5 6 7 8 9 - ,
Q W E . T Y I U O P
Z S D F G H J K L M
A X & C V B N ? ; R

Remington made several adjustments, and launched the Sholes and Glidden typewriter on July 1, 1874.[3] Its keyboard layout was almost the same QWERTY keyboard layout we use today, with a few minor differences. 1 and 0 were left out to help shave down production costs, on the basis that these numerals could be produced using other keys, such as a capital I and a capital O. Remington also swapped the R and . keys.

The 0 was added fairly early on, but some keyboards well into the 1970s[4] were still missing a 1.

When this was launched to the world, it took a while to sell, and needed some polishing in terms of the overall product before it hit a fit with the market:

The first Remington typewriter sold poorly (it could only type in upper-case letters, was expensive at $125 per unit, and often broke). The updated Remington 2 typewriter, introduced in 1878, changed this. Not only did it remedy some of the defects of the Sholes and Glidden machine, the launch allowed Remington to sell the typewriter business[5] to three former employees. Bringing marketing expertise to bear, the new Remington Standard Type-writer Company[6] was able to bring the typewriter to commercial success.

However, now (in 2017) we still use a QWERTY keyboard. We still teach QWERTY in our schools. And generally, no one questions how it was designed, who it was designed for, and why we still use the 1870 model almost 150 years later.

What Happens When the World Changes?

There are at least six different keyboard layouts[7] that are well-known enough to have a Wikipedia page. Of these six, Dvorak is the one that has a small following of people that have run studies and research to show the benefits of this model over QWERTY:

Though Dvorak may sound like another string of letters, it's in fact the sur-name of this keyboard layout's inventor, August Dvorak. The inventor felt, when he patented his design in 1936, that QWERTY was uneconomical and uncomfortable—and therefore wasn't the perfect layout. Dvorak believed that his layout was more efficient, and studies seem to agree.

People using QWERTY keyboards only make 32 percent of strokes on the "home row" (where your fingers naturally rest on a keyboard). For Dvorak, that rises to 70 percent. And likewise, most people are right handed: Dvorak accounts for that, making more than half the strokes right handed. QWERTY calls on people to use their left hands more. But save for a few eager practi-tioners, Dvorak is the lesser-known layout.

Regardless of the benefits of Dvorak, people do not want to change when stuck in comfortable habits that work well enough.

We can see a very similar pattern with our education system. Our cur-rent model was designed years ago with specific purposes in mind. A lot has stayed the same since that design including:

1. When we go to school, and when we have breaks from school.
2. Hours learning per day.
3. Subject areas.
4. Grade levels.

This list could go on, but I think you get the point. QWERTY was designed for a different world and different purpose, and although it still works fine (as I currently type on my QWERTY keyboard), that doesn't mean it is the best solution.

There are many schools and districts that are moving away from a "tradi-tional" education experience. In pockets across the US and the world, things are changing, yet the majority of our schools function in an eerily similar way to a 19th century model.

In the design thinking process, there is a piece that we often forget to continue with after launching it out into the world: iteration.

If we don't consistently iterate, we will consistently fall behind.

After launching to the world it brings us back to a place where we can look, listen, and learn again.

Iteration takes time. Revising and editing takes time. Adjusting takes time. Modeling and taking risks all are time consuming activities that don't always follow a typical scope and sequence of a curriculum.

Making the time to rethink our purpose, to come up with new ideas, and then trial and pilot them to see if they work, all takes time.

But that time is necessary to innovation. It's hard to create new ideas that work without time to make them work.

The QWERTY keyboard was developed for a mechanical device that had problems with keys getting stuck. With digital devices we don't have to worry about that problem any more.

Our educational system was developed for a time period of agriculture lifestyle and industrial growth. We aren't preparing the majority of our students to work in fields or in factories any more. So let's look and learn about possible solutions to make it a better process.

Making Time for Iteration

My daughter lowered her eyes, looked at me, and said, "I can't do it."

I looked back and asked her again to put one foot on the board, push off with her other foot, and then put that foot on the board when she was moving.

She was being a typical 6-year old who was trying to learn how to ride a skateboard.

"No," she said. "I'm not doing this any more. Can you push me?"

It would have been easy for me to help her get both feet on the board and give her a push to get her started, but I had already done that. And now, after guiding her through the process (and almost falling myself while demonstrating) it was time for her to keep trying if she wanted to make any progress.

I told her "no" and asked for her to try again, this time focusing on getting a good push so she could be moving when she put her foot back on the board.

She was visibly upset. She knew that I could help her out. I knew that I could help her out. But in her mind she didn't see the bigger picture. She didn't realize that only by trying—and failing—herself, would she ever be able to ride a skateboard without my help.

The Teaching Dilemma

As parents and teachers, we have a continual dilemma with our children and students. We have this same dilemma when we are helping colleagues or others in the workplace as well.

There will be many times when you can easily help someone achieve a certain level of success by doing the work for them. For our children, this can be holding their hands while they learn to walk. For our students, this can be giving a formulaic graphic organizer for writing an essay.

We have the choice to allow for failure and provide support,[8] or do it for them and make it easier on both of us.

Jessica Lahey[9] wrote an article in 2013 on *Why Parents Need to Let Their Children Fail*[10] that went on to say:

> *This is what we teachers see most often: what the authors term 'high responsiveness and low demandingness' parents. These parents are highly responsive to the perceived needs and issues of their children, and don't give their children the chance to solve their own problems. These parents 'rush to school at the whim of a phone call from their child to deliver items such as forgotten lunches, forgotten assignments, forgotten uniforms' and 'demand better grades on the final semester reports or threaten withdrawal from school'.*

The study mentioned by Lahey[11] describes the problem that over-parenting has on our children, and the impact it causes in the learning process.

I'd ask the question if we are too guilty of "over-teaching" and enabling students in the learning process so that they lean on the help of adults, instead of figuring it out themselves.

The Gift of Failure

Lahey's book, *The Gift of Failure*,[12] offers some critical research on why letting students figure it out is better for them in the moment, in their future, and in their understanding of what learning can look like. In fact, letting our children "figure it out" on their own is one of the most empowering ways to give them ownership of their lives and learning path. This notion drove my interaction with my daughter to be very different than it might have usually ended up.

After we finished our short back-and-forth conversation, my daughter hopped on the skateboard and took off down our driveway. She got both feet on the skateboard and was moving fast. Then . . . almost like out of a movie, she tried to stop and flew off the back of the board.

I tried to play off the fall by congratulating her by getting both feet on the board. It didn't help. She was upset and blamed me for the fall off the board. But the next day she was back on, then trying to figure out how to stop. Learning, it seems, is contagious: as long as we let our children and students go through the entire process and support along the way as best we can.

Notes

1 www.typewritermuseum.org/history/inventors_sholes.html.
2 www.cnet.com/news/a-brief-history-of-the-qwerty-keyboard.
3 www.branchcollective.org/?ps_articles=christopher-keep-the-introduction-of-the-sholes-glidden-type-writer-1874.
4 www.mrmartinweb.com/type.htm#olivetti.
5 https://en.wikipedia.org/wiki/Clarence_Seamans.
6 http://americanhistory.si.edu/collections/search/object/nmah_850053.
7 http://mentalfloss.com/article/52483/6-non-qwerty-keyboard-layouts.
8 http://ajjuliani.com/10-ways-differentiate-choice.
9 www.jessicalahey.com/the-gift-of-failure.
10 www.theatlantic.com/national/archive/2013/01/why-parents-need-to-let-their-children-fail/272603.
11 http://eprints.qut.edu.au/55005.
12 Lahey, J. (2015) *The Gift of Failure: How the Best Parents Learn to Let Go So Their Children Can Succeed*. New York: HarperCollins.

Chapter Reflection

What ideas resonated with you from this chapter? Take notes, draw, brainstorm, and reflect in the space below. Share your ideas on Twitter using the hashtag #beintentional.

10

Allowing for the New and Unknown

New Is Always Happening

In 1939, audiences around the United States were delighted when the black and white scenery of *The Wizard of Oz* completely transformed into full technicolor in the blink of an eye. The film was not the first to introduce color, but it is widely regarded as one of the first to popularize color motion pictures. Interestingly, *The Wizard of Oz* was a flop at the box office. It was critically acclaimed and written about in newspapers—especially for this innovative use of color—but did not make much money, nor draw a wide audience, in its initial release.

Fifteen years later something interesting happened. Something that would lead to *The Wizard of Oz* becoming known as one of the all-time great films, as we believe it to be today: the attention and eyeballs of millions of Americans were focused on television. On November 3rd, 1956, CBS aired *The Wizard of Oz* for the first time on television. It was an immediate hit and one that soon became an annual tradition. Millions of Americans would get together as families each year to watch *The Wizard of Oz*.

During this period in time, something else interesting was happening that sparked such a love for *The Wizard of Oz*. The transition to technicolor years earlier had wowed those that went to the movie theater to see the film, but in 1956 there weren't many (all but a few) color television sets. However, over the next 10–15 years, color televisions began to pop up in households across the country, and often people's first visual experience on a color television would be the annual broadcast of *The Wizard of Oz*. Millions of children grew up with this movie becoming a cherished family moment that not only brought them into the world of color television, but also enhanced the story in their minds forever.

So although the innovation of technicolor had happened years earlier, until *The Wizard of Oz* engaged the minds of many, the movie (and its innovative use of color) was never fully appreciated.

It's All About Attention

This pattern can be seen time and time again when sharing the stories of innovative breakthroughs and experiences. Often, the technological feat and innovative work takes place months, years, and decades before it is accepted and paid attention to by the general public.

Engagement only happens when there is high attention. So regardless of the innovative work or practice, if the attention isn't there then engagement won't show up either.

The creators of *The Wizard of Oz* may have set out to make a movie that would stand the test of time and become a family classic. But for over 15 years after its release, this was not the case. It was only after their film, and its burst of color, was shown to a national audience on television (not the format they originally set out to have it on) did it receive enough attention to engage at a high level.

It's Interesting to See This Happen In Education As Well

I was once at a conference in Hershey, Pennsylvania (PETE&C), listening to George Couros[1] give a Keynote on *The Innovator's Mindset* (great book if you haven't checked it out yet).[2] Sitting with my colleagues in the audience I could sense every time George struck a nerve and connected with the people in attendance. His stories were personal and moving, but it was often the way he told the story with technology that engaged. Mixing videos, pictures, and sound together to bring the audience into the actual experience he was describing made for an entertaining talk.

There was one moment, however, that stuck out for me. Toward the end of the talk George shared a moment where he thought he may have lost control of a young audience. The experience centered around the use of Twitter and, as I looked around the room, everyone knew what he was talking about.

I immediately flashed back to six years prior when I first met George: he was one of the people that actively got me started in using Twitter to share, connect, and learn. If he had shared this same story six years ago, many people would have been wondering what he was talking about. A few would have been on the social network, or heard about Twitter in the news, but most would be at a loss in understanding the technology would be a barrier to connecting with the story.

In this moment, the audience was engaged. It resonated with many personal experiences we had each had as teachers and leaders. When he shared this quote from a student, it immediately made us all think:

Figure 10.1

"Social media is like water bacause it is everywhere in our life. We can ignore it and watch kids drown, or we can teach kids how to swim. Which way are going to go?"

–From a student (@gcouros; http://georgecouros.ca/lblog/archives/5267)

Where Is Our Students' Attention? Where Are They Already Engaging?

It's easy for us to say we are "never going to get on Instagram" or "never going to use Snapchat"—just like we said we were never going to use Facebook or Twitter—but we would be missing a huge opportunity to actually engage with our students and use this innovation (new social networks) to connect with their attention.

It would have been easy for the creators of *The Wizard of Oz* to sit back and say, "This film was made for the big screen. It would lose its impact if it was on a small television. And what about the technicolor? These TVs don't even have color as an option."

Instead, they took their story and message to the platform (and networks) that had the most attention. In doing so they connected with a new generation and let their story spread farther than they could have ever imagined.

I've got news for you. The social networks of Snapchat, Instagram, Facebook, and Twitter are today's (2017) versions of the ABC, NBC, and CBS networks of 1967. That's where the attention is. We cannot wish it away. We cannot go back. And in a few years, it will change again. That's the reality in which we are living, learning, and teaching.

When we see innovation as a way to connect with students and engage through platforms, tools, and networks where their attention is already placed, we earn the opportunity to share our message farther and deeper than we might ever have imagined.

It's OK to Say "I Don't Know"

When our students or peers don't know something, they are either going to find out by skimming something online, or talking to a real person that actually has the knowledge. My question is this: **why do we make it so hard on students and peers to say "I don't know"?**

A Larger Cultural Problem with Faking What You Know

Karl Taro Greenfeld, a journalist and author, published an op-ed in the *New York Times* on faking cultural literacy.[3]

It's never been so easy to pretend to know so much without actually knowing anything. We pick topical, relevant bits from Facebook, Twitter, or emailed news alerts, and then regurgitate them. Instead of watching *Mad Men* or the Super Bowl or the Oscars or a presidential debate, you can simply scroll through someone else's live-tweeting of it, or read the recaps the next day. Our cultural canon is becoming determined by whatever gets the most clicks.

I do this so often that I'm at a loss for words. How many of us have:

1. Tweeted out or shared an article after only reading half-way through?
2. Discussed a show or TV event with co-workers the next day when we were really fast asleep the night before?
3. Input commentary on a book, movie, or TV show that we never watched, but "read" some reviews on?

You know what my daughter would say in any of these situations? **I don't know.**

One of my favorite writers on this planet, Shane Parrish, wrote a follow-up story to the NYT piece. In his article, *Why it's never been easier to fake what you know*,[4] Shane digs a bit deeper into this problem and how it actually impacts our lives:

> *I was talking to Ryan Holiday about this and he said, 'It's not bad because it's dishonest. It's bad because we make real, sometimes life altering decisions based on this fakery.' Unable to discern between what we know and what we pretend to know, we ultimately become victims of our own laziness and intellectual dishonesty.*

What are we doing to ourselves, our students, our peers, and our children when we "fake what we know"? Wouldn't it be so much better if we could all say, "I don't know" without worrying what the ramifications might be—personally or professionally—for not understanding something or not being able to offer an opinion.

A Simple Solution for Education

I'm going to come out and say this: *I don't really know* how to fix this problem culturally. It seems to be growing. It seems to be expected now, and I'm not sure that is ever going to change in the era of smart watches and glasses and Siri. Maybe there will be a pendulum swing and people will get tired of these fake conversations where everyone has an opinion about everything.

But, as an educator and learner, there is something simple we can do to bring back "I don't know" into the learning process: **model it ourselves as teachers and leaders**.

When we don't know something in a staff meeting, we should say so. When a student asks a question we don't know the answer to, we should learn it together as a class. Just as failure is a huge part of the learning process, so too is the honesty to admit when you don't know.

Shane Parrish continues his thoughts on what this means:

> *It means you can't skim and pretend. It means you actually have to do the work. It means you have to be honest with yourself. It means you have to know when you're operating in your circle of competence and when you're outside of it. It means you have to criticize yourself. It means you need to know the other side to whatever point you're trying to make better than the other person. It means you have to say 'I don't know'.*

We are fast moving into a time of education where information is not just at our fingertips, but on the tip of our tongue. Ask and you shall receive (information, that is). Yet if we really want students to make an impact on this world, they'll need to truly know what they are talking about. They'll also need to seriously care about what they do in life, instead of caring about sounding informed in every discussion.

I'm hoping my daughter keeps saying "I don't know" as she goes through our educational system. I'm not sure if this is wishful thinking, but I also hope I'm able to admit when I don't know and keep from "faking cultural literacy", in order to model this for my own kids.

Will we ever get to a place where it's OK again to admit you didn't understand, or need more time to process?

I don't know.

What Happens When We Allow for the New and Unknown

I sensed the anticipation as soon as I entered the classroom. Groups of students were huddled together flipping through notes and documentation. A few were going back and forth about what they were going to say. As I headed to the whiteboard a hush fell over the room and one student asked, "Do we get the whole class period Mr. J?"

It was first marking period, "Appeals Day", in my 9th grade English class. And it was the first time my students had ever been told they would be allowed to argue for their grades.

The bell rang and I answered, "Yes, you get the whole class period. Remember how this is structured and how you should act. The first 10 minutes are for you to organize your appeals." Students gathered together to make sure they were ready, as I waited for the arguments to begin.

My View on Grades Changed

As a new teacher, I was told time and time again not to give in to students who argued about grades. I was told they were complainers and would never be happy. Yet after almost every assessment, I had questions from students about their grades. At first I took this personally, acting as if a student asking about a test question was an attack on my professional abilities. I look back embarrassed on how I handled these situations.

The reality is that many teachers still act like this. They treat tests and assessments as sacred documents that should never be questioned. My mindset changed during a grad school class in which our professor conferenced with each student about our grades. He told us to come prepared to defend how we were assessed. I was confused . . . but also happy to have a discussion about what I understood, and where I could have done better throughout the class.

To me, we can treat assessments and grades in two different ways:

1. Grades are payment for work performed, much like a salary.
2. Grades are a reflection of how well a student demonstrates their ability/understanding, much like playing time on an athletic team.

If you treat grades like a salary, shouldn't students be able to argue and fight for a better salary if they can prove they deserve it?

If you treat grades like playing time, shouldn't students have a chance to show their ability beyond one practice/game?

My solution for our class was an end of the marking period, "Appeals Day", where students could craft a defense of their grades and propose changes based on real evidence—not just their opinion.

Here's the handout I gave them in the beginning of the Marking Period about Appeals Day:

Appeals Day

Overview

First and foremost, Appeals Day is a privilege. Remember this as you can lose a privilege at any time. During Appeals Day you have the ability to give reasons or cite evidence in support of an answer with the aim of persuading me to change your grade. There are no guarantees, regardless of how impressive your argument may be. That being said, Appeals Day does present a real opportunity to improve your grade, if you follow the rules and expectations.

Expectations

- ◆ You will be respectful.
- ◆ You will come prepared.
- ◆ You will be patient.
- ◆ You will accept my final decision.
- ◆ You will follow the rules.

Rules

1. The first 10 minutes of class will be a time for you and your class-mates to organize your appeals.
2. The rest of the class and I will hear your appeals.
3. The largest appeals (amount of people appealing) will begin first, and work down till there are only individual appeals remaining.
4. When appealing you must present the following information in a respectful manner: the assignment/paper/assessment, the question/ area of concern, your given grade, what the problem is with your given grade, supporting evidence for your claim, what you believe your grade should be changed to.

5. After you present your appeal, I will provide my ruling. You will have one more chance to retort before the final verdict is made. Once the final verdict is made you must accept the decision and make room for the next appeal.

I hope you all enjoy Appeals Day as much as I do, and we can continue this end-of-the-marking period tradition throughout the school year.

The End Result

Appeals Day became an end-of-the-marking period staple in my classes, and students loved the ability to argue, with evidence, for their grades. Many students received points back, and many didn't get anything except a "good try" from me and their classmates. But the points weren't the point.

Appeals Day was a success because it shifted how my students viewed grades. Instead of them seeing grades as a fixed, one-time assessment on their learning, it gave students ownership over their grades, and how they accepted assessments on their abilities.

Although many of my fellow teachers thought I was crazy for running Appeals Day each marking period, it also cut down all the complaining that used to happen before, about assessments and grades. Parents called in less about their children's grades, and it was an open and transparent process.

The biggest benefit was how hard my students collaborated and worked to prepare for Appeals Day. They enjoyed it. And I never once said they *had* to collaborate; they did it out of purpose and necessity.

Notes

1 http://georgecouros.ca.
2 http://ajjuliani.com/how-to-develop-an-innovators-mindset-at-your-school.
3 www.nytimes.com/2014/05/25/opinion/sunday/faking-cultural-literacy. html?_r=1.
4 http://betabeat.com/2014/06/the-era-of-fake-knowledge-why-its-never-been-easier-to-fake-what-you-know.

Chapter Reflection

What ideas resonated with you from this chapter? Take notes, draw, brainstorm, and reflect in the space below. Share your ideas on Twitter using the hashtag #beintentional.

Part 3

Doing the Work

11

Guiding Risk-Taking

In 11th grade I decided to try out for the school musical. I'd never been involved in a school drama or musical, and spent most of my time playing varsity football and basketball.

I ended up being chosen to play the part of the Lion in *The Wizard of Oz*. Talk about embarrassing! I heard it loud and clear from some friends and family who thought I was crazy. Luckily, most of the people in my life were supportive and I followed through with the performance.

After our three shows I felt great about taking the risk to try out and play the part of the Cowardly Lion. It was an awesome experience, and we had a lot of fun along the way. Yet, I remember a specific comment about the show from one of my peers in class that called it "a joke".

Not the actual show, but the fact that I had gone out for the play and was the Lion. Amidst all the positive feedback, I couldn't help but focus on the one criticism I heard . . .

Times Have Changed, But My Reaction to Critical Feedback Has Stayed Relatively the Same

After its release, I received a critical review on my book, *Inquiry and Innovation in the Classroom*,[1] on Amazon.

At first, I tried to brush it off. I've heard from so many amazing teachers and leaders who have read the book, or my blog, and given positive feedback.

In fact, that same day I had some great emails come in talking about "solving the biggest problem in education" at a workshop activity.

But I couldn't let it go. The review nagged at me. After a couple of days, I reached out to a few authors and asked them how they deal with negative reviews. Each had similar stories and talked about the feeling of pouring so much time and energy into a book, and then hearing critical feedback.

What came away from those conversations were a few truths about dealing with criticism that I've thought about:

1. When You Take Risks, Criticism Will Follow

If you sit in your office, or classroom, or house and rarely come out . . . you will probably stay clear of criticism. Any time you decide to take a different viewpoint on a subject, write something for the world to see, or ask questions that no one is asking . . . you are taking a risk.

There are millions of people who live their lives avoiding risk. I personally can't be one of them. I've tried to "slow down" or "follow the course" but it never works out. And when you take risks, criticism will follow. In fact, I'd go as far as saying that if no one is criticizing your work, then it might not be worth it.

In this situation, I have to remember who I am as a person. Then I realize that the risks I take have to be worth the criticism that will follow.

2. Don't Dismiss All Criticism; Take it for What it Is

I talked with someone who gave me great advice: the criticism you receive can often have some truth.

This hit home.

It's easy to dismiss criticism or feedback that you don't like . . . but if you look at it from another perspective, it can be helpful. This doesn't mean you take everything at face value, but realize that it's worth taking a look at what the feedback suggests about your work.

This is easier said than done!

3. Keeping it to Yourself Is Not Going to Help

I've gone full circle on this topic. I thought for a long time that you should keep criticism and feedback to yourself, because who wants to hear about it? (Sorry!) Then I reached out and started sharing some stories and realized that almost everyone who is creating, writing, or putting their thoughts and ideas down for the world to see has dealt with criticism.

Now, I've gone from keeping it to myself to sharing it on my blog—and in this book—with the world. Here's my thought: it didn't help to keep it to myself, so I'm seeing if being open about it changes anything.

I do know that talking about it and hearing about other situations did open my eyes to a greater understanding of what it means to take risks, create, and handle yourself professionally in any context.

4. Add Fuel to Your Creative Fire

If you are a person who takes risks and makes/creates things, there has to be something that lights your fire. Criticism works wonderfully as a motivator.

It has led me to really focus on making my next book the best it can be, and an extremely practical and helpful book for teachers and anyone in education.

The truth is, you can never please everyone. And if you try to please everyone you'll end up helping no one.

So you have to focus that energy and creative fire on making something of value for your intended audience. When that audience grows, or shifts, or changes . . . there are going to be new voices that may want a different type of product than you've created.

My final thought is this: are you doing good work, with good people, for good reasons?

If you can answer yes to each of those points, then push forward because the world needs your voice . . . regardless of the feedback you may receive along the way.

The Good Work

As I work with students and teachers there is one common thread that the "stand-out" classrooms share: **they take risks**. Not only do these students and teachers take learning risks, but they also take them *together*. They are partners in the learning process, where the teacher is the "lead learner".

My job as a staff developer let me see hundreds of classrooms, where before I usually only saw my own. It inspired me to be a risk-taker in my own job, and to share the risks that my teachers are taking, with the world. Here's some of the favorite ways I see my teachers and students taking risks, ways anyone can do the same with their class:

1. Give a Fresh Start

As teachers we often get a ton of information about our students before they walk in the door: past test scores, socio-economic background, behavior issues in other classes, etc. Some of this information is very important (I'm thinking about IEPs) but none of this information should make us start our relationship with our students based on assumptions.

Each school year should begin with a fresh start. Each marking period should renew that fresh start. If we start our relationship with assumptions instead of hope, we've already made a mess of the learning experience.

2. Student Choice

I'm obviously a huge advocate for 20% Time[2] and Genius Hour[3] in the classroom. I believe inquiry-driven learning experiences and projects allow students to "have a say" in their learning path.[4] However, I've heard from many teachers who say they don't have the time to run a fully fledged 20% Time project in their class. That's OK.

Make sure you still give your students choice in what they learn and how they learn it. I know it can be risky at first. You'll feel like maybe you've abandoned the curriculum (is that such a bad thing?). You'll feel like you've given up some control (is that such a bad thing?). However, what you've really done is allowed the students to motivate their own learning. It's a risk, for sure . . . but it is one worth taking.

3. Looking at Data Together

There will be data. Lots of it. And if we keep all the data to ourselves, then we are doing the students a huge disservice. If we truly believe that our tests are valid and important learning measures, then we should meet with students 1-on-1 to show the previous results and areas where they struggle.

I did this as an 11th grade teacher and it opened up some great conversations about testing and data. It also pointed out some areas that helped me to help my students. For instance, most of my students struggled with vocabulary. Maybe the "old me" would have taken this upon himself to ramp up vocab units and quizzes. But after talking with my students it was apparent that they didn't understand vocabulary "context clues". Now I could teach them context clues and they would be able to read books, stories, and non-fiction that they actually enjoyed.

Don't make data the enemy. Instead, try to use it for what it's worth and make it a collaborative learning experience.

4. Let Them Teach

Have you ever thought about giving your students the reigns on a class assignment? I know that my personal experience shows that when I teach something, I learn much more about it. The same goes for our students. I'm sure you already have projects and assignments in class where students are put into "expert groups". Maybe you do a jigsaw activity, where students then present what they know to other students . Why not take it a step further and let them create a mini-lesson on their expert content. They'll have to create an activity, build handouts, and present to the class as a lead learner. Students find this challenging, but also rewarding.

5. Go on a Mission and Skip Class

Field trips can sometimes sound boring. Or they don't have much to do with actual learning. Instead go on a mission with your class. Present a guiding question, and then go on a hunt for answers! The 9th graders at my school don't just learn about pH values, they go on a mission. We take them to the local watershed where they spend an entire day taking measurements and figuring out why a particular area of our community floods, and the type of damage that happens when waste and toxins are mixed with our water supply. They leave knowing more about "science" than any lesson could ever teach them.

6. Learn Something New Together

If you are a teacher, chances are you know your curriculum and content inside-and-out. Yet there has to be something that you want to learn more about. When you learn something "new" with your class they get to see you as a "lead learner" and not just the teacher who has all the answers. They see how you ask questions, experiment with options, and use your curiosity to guide a learning path.

Plus, they get to help out along the way and show you a different perspective on the learning experience. Learning something new together is a great community builder, but also an amazing way to model life-long learning.

7. Read for Reading's Sake

Aren't you tired of all the "reasons" we have to "read" in school? I know I am. Sometimes I want our students to understand that reading can be a pleasurable activity with no other outcome other than being entertained. We tend to do some of this type of reading in the younger grades, but as students get older, our view on reading gets colder—like that rhyme?!

Let's change that and take the time (and risk) to read for reading's sake. Reader's workshops are a perfect opportunity to give students time, and permission, to read for pleasure. Also, how about we make summer reading about *enjoying* a book and not forcing a text on all of our students? Just a thought.

8. Build/Make Something Useful Together

I'm not the most "hands on" learner. I was awful in shop class and even got stitches in my thumb after using a saw in high school! But there is a rush I get from trying to make something. I also learn something new every time I build, fix, or make. Most of my "making" has been done on a computer and online, which is fine. Yet there is a risk that many teachers think they are doing "making" by handing out a project.

The problem with many projects is the lack of use and purpose. Why make something that is either going to end up in the trash can, or on the fridge for a week before the trash can? And digital projects are the same. Are you spending time creating "digital fridge art" with your students?

Instead, take the risk to create/build/make something useful together with your students. Something that is going to last. Something that will help your school, your community, or even the world. Then your students will understand that real "pride" in your work isn't limited to what you make, but instead the reason you made it.

9. Tell Them Your Story—Listen to Their Stories

It's the first day of school. You tell your students a little bit about yourself and your background. Then they tell you, and each other, about their story. Maybe you even have them create a little project about themselves. Flash forward to March. You haven't spent much time at all talking about your story, and when is the last time you heard about their stories?

I've fallen into this trap before, and then when I ask myself where the connection is with my students, I realize . . . we haven't shared our stories.

When we write about our stories, talk about our stories, and help each other out, that's when the real connection happens; learning becomes a communal experience instead of an individual experience. Don't be afraid to share your story and ask your students to share theirs.

10. Blog Together

This is risky, I know. Putting your thoughts and ideas out to the world . . . and letting your students share their thoughts and ideas out in the world. But it's totally worth it.

When you blog with your students you take the interaction from class and put it into a forum where anyone can participate. If you use platforms like Kidblog and Edublogs it is easy to create a safe blogging experience for your students (take that risk off the table). Too often we want to keep what happens in our classes hidden, like it is some secret learning laboratory. Yet, most of the great teachers I know spend time sharing with the world what their students are doing. Blogging is the easiest way to do that.

These risks aren't really risks at all. Instead, they are choices. Do you want to keep doing things the same way with your class, or do you want to grow as a lead learner beside your students? Choose wisely.

Notes

1 http://ajjuliani.com/books/inquiry-innovation-classroom.
2 http://ajjuliani.com/the-20-project-like-google-in-my-class.
3 http://ajjuliani.com/genius-hour-whats-it-all-about.
4 http://ajjuliani.com/choice-learning.

Chapter Reflection

What ideas resonated with you from this chapter? Take notes, draw, brainstorm, and reflect in the space below. Share your ideas on Twitter using the hashtag #beintentional.

12

Celebrating Failing and Learning

While John Spencer and I were developing the LAUNCH Cycle,[1] we came up with a few areas that were likely stumbling blocks in the creative (design-thinking inspired) process. One of the keys to the LAUNCH Cycle is taking the time to **Look, Listen, and Learn** throughout the entire process—that is the **L** in the LAUNCH acronym.

In talking with a mentor about the LAUNCH Cycle we had a good conversation about when it was appropriate to share that learning. The quick answer: all the time. From start to finish you can be learning and sharing during the process. Whether it is students doing a Genius Hour Project, teachers creating their own PD, or school leaders implementing an initiative—the key is to be transparent with that learning process.

Here's the Problem: To Be Transparent and Share Your Learning Means to Open Yourself up to Public Failures

This is true for all of us. It is one of the biggest stumbling blocks in the creative process. And it's not the failing; it's the resiliency to get back up and keep trying. It's the tenacity to continue attacking the problem and developing solutions. It's the feeling that your work is not complete until you've made some sort of progress.

And I know what you are saying right now, because I'm saying the same thing: it's one thing to fail and bounce back myself, or in a small group.

It's a completely different level to fail in front of what seems like the whole world and try to keep going in the creative process!

But if we want to be great, if we want our students to be great, if we want our schools to be great, then failure, and sharing that failure, has to be a part of the process. It cannot be hidden. It cannot be swept under the rug. It cannot be forgotten.

I'm right there with you. I need to learn how to fail better, and bounce back stronger, and not be afraid to share it with the world. For me, it gets me inspired to hear and see others sharing epic failures with an audience. Enter my inspiration: Elon Musk.

Learning How to Fail from Elon Musk

One of the best lessons on sharing how failure is part of the design-thinking process is happening right now, in front of our eyes on public display. We are living in an amazing time, where every step of SpaceX's program is being broadcast, shared, and discussed in real-time. If you aren't sure what I'm talking about, here's the general idea.[2]

Elon Musk was a co-founder of PayPal, where he made millions of dollars when the company was sold to eBay. Instead of buying yachts and living off his riches, Musk decided on tackling three of the biggest problems he could think of: dependence on fossil fuels, space travel, and solar energy. He formed three companies: Tesla is the car company that makes electric cars and battery gigafactories; SolarCity is the smallest company, founded on bringing solar energy to the masses; and then there is SpaceX.

SpaceX has brought the Space Race back into the 21st century. Musk's goal is to eventually have a SpaceX team travel to Mars. And he is not joking about this. They are hitting almost every milestone along the way. But the best part of this entire story is that we get to watch it live. The ups and downs, wins and failures. It's an awesome design-thinking process happening right in front of our eyes.

In 2005, when he was starting out on this journey with SpaceX, Musk said the following:

Figure 12.1

> **"Failure is an option here. If things are not failing, you are not innovating enough."**
>
> –Elon Musk (in interview with Fast Company, February 2005)

Failure has been a huge part of SpaceX's ethos since the beginning. In fact, it almost failed its way out of business.

2006: First launch—failure

2007: Second launch—failure

2008: Third launch—failure

It only had enough money and resources left for one more launch. It needed to be successful in order to get any type of funding. Here's what happened.

A friend of Musk, Adeo Ressi, describes it like this:

Everything hinged on that launch . . . If it works, epic success. If it fails—if one thing goes differently and it fails—epic failure. No in between. No partial credit. He'd had three failures already. It would have been over. We're talking Harvard Business School case study—rich guy who goes into the rocket business and loses it all.

But on September 28, 2008, SpaceX set off the fourth launch—and nailed it. It put a dummy payload into orbit without a hitch, becoming only the second privately-funded company ever to do so.

Falcon 1 was also the most cost-efficient rocket ever to launch—priced at $7.9 million, it cost less than a third of the best US alternative at the time.

NASA took notice. The successful fourth launch was enough evidence for it that SpaceX was worth trusting, and at the end of 2008 NASA called Musk and told him they wanted to offer SpaceX a $1.6 billion contract to make 12 deliveries for it to the ISS.

Notice, that all of these failures were very public. Livestreamed online. Written about in the mass media. Talked about among colleagues and employees at SpaceX.

Then notice something else: you probably didn't know about any of this. One of the biggest lessons we can learn from Elon Musk about failing and bouncing back publicly is that even though you may share it with the world, it doesn't have to be humiliating. Musk and SpaceX failed proudly. It meant they were taking risks. It meant they were pushing forward and trying to make a better world.

As teachers and leaders we can often feel defeated when we try something new, take a risk, and end up not getting the results we hoped for. Yet if we share that journey we are inspiring others to take action themselves. We are showing the world that we aren't "settling" for what we have, but are actively working for something better.

Musk on the Fundamental Problem with Taking Risks

SpaceX has continued to fail since that successful launch. But with each failure (and with each success) it grows stronger as a company which practices resiliency and promotes risk-taking. Its latest risk is trying to land a rocket (that goes into orbit) onto a landing pad in the middle of the ocean. They have successfully landed a rocket on land, but for bigger launches they need the flexibility of landing the rocket on a robot boat at sea.

So far it's had four attempts. All failures. Three were close; one not at all. Now, as it goes for its fifth attempt, articles like this one from Wired Magazine are popping up all over the internet: Watch SpaceX Rocket (Probably) Crash Into a Robot Boat (Again).[3]

But for SpaceX this is how it functions. Failure is a part of the process. Let's take a look at the LAUNCH Cycle to see how it is sharing, taking risks, learning, and failing throughout this process.

L: Look, Listen, and Learn

In the first phase, SpaceX (including Musk) looks at past experiences, listens to experts, and learns from each other about its next mission or launch. This isn't always pretty or easy. It's a lot of hard work to learn at a deep level, and you can miss things along the way.

A: Ask Tons of Questions

Now filled with a general understanding, it asks questions and dives deeper into its mission. Why didn't this work? Why did this system fail? Asking questions helps to get to the next step.

U: Understanding the Process and/or Problem

This leads to understanding the process or problem through experiences. Here SpaceX is failing and learning through those failures. It is also sharing with its team so everyone can be informed and get a deeper level of understanding.

N: Navigate Ideas

The SpaceX team now applies that newly acquired knowledge to potential solutions. In this phase, the team navigates ideas. Here the team not only brainstorms, but also analyzes ideas, combines ideas, and generates a concept for what it will create.

C: Create a Prototype

In this next phase, it creates a prototype. There may be many prototypes. It could be a rocket, or a system for landing, or a way to use less fuel. Creation happens, with failure often expected to be the initial result.

H: Highlight and Fix

Next, it begins to highlight what's working and fix what's failing. The goal here is to view this revision process as an experiment full of iterations, where every mistake takes it closer to success. This is happening right now at SpaceX by launching four times and failing four times. It continues to highlight, tweak, and fix.

This is not easy when you are first starting to take risks. It may feel like the whole world is against you. It may feel like everyone thinks you are crazy. As a teacher or school leader you may be saying, "If I try something and fail, I'll never be allowed to take a creative risk again."

Musk dealt with similar sanctions and possibilities when he was starting SpaceX and trying to figure out how to deal with the regulators. Regulators controlled how many "risks" you could take and what the ramifications were if you failed and messed up along the way.

But in Musk's mind, the problem was not with the regulators themselves, but the entire system put in place. He points this out in one particular quote:

> There is a fundamental problem with regulators. If a regulator agrees to change a rule and something bad happens, they can easily lose their career. Whereas if they change a rule and something good happens, they don't even get a reward. So, it's very asymmetric. It's then very easy to understand why regulators resist changing the rules. It's because there's a big punishment on one side and no reward on the other. How would any rational person behave in such a scenario?

The situation he's talking about is loss aversion[4] (as we mentioned earlier). As Shane Parrish says:

> It doesn't stop at regulators, it extends into other areas as well. The same principle applies to most CEOs, managers, leaders, and teachers. If you want to predict behavior, take a close look at the incentives.

Let's change the wording in that paragraph for school leaders and teacher scenario . . .

There is a fundamental problem with *teachers/leaders*. If a *teacher/leader* agrees to change a rule and something bad happens, they can easily lose their career. Whereas if they change a rule and something good happens, they don't even get a reward. So, it's very asymmetric. It's then very easy to understand why *teachers/leaders* resist changing the rules. It's because there's a big punishment on one side and no reward on the other. How would any rational *teacher/leader* behave in such a scenario?

Does this sound eerily familiar? It's not necessarily any teacher, or school leader, or student's fault for not taking risks. Often it's based on the system that is in place. **When a system actively punishes risk-takers, there tends to be fewer of them.**

So, is that it? Should we give up, throw our hands in the air and say, "Well, I guess there is nothing we can do!"

Yes, that's an option. It's an option many of us take when we feel like we are beaten down, frustrated, and overwhelmed with the current reality of a system that punishes risks and failure. But, I believe there is another way to think about taking risks. One that provides a more hopeful outcome.

As Elon Musk says*:*

If something is important enough, you should try, even if the probable outcome is failure.

How to Take Risks in a System Not Built for Them

The first thing we can learn from Elon Musk on taking risks is to not do it alone. Sure, Musk put all of his own money on the line, and started his companies by himself, but he has always built and consulted with a *team* when taking a risk. Whether it was talking to every rocket scientist and NASA engineer he could find, or consulting with former aerospace experts, Musk decided to take a risk, then brought a team together to make it happen. This team may not be in your own school or space—it may be online and from around the world—but you need support to pull it off.

The second piece of advice is make sure to *research and plan* to the best of your abilities. If you take a risk and "wing it", chances are people won't take you, or your work, seriously. However, if you have a plan backed by research and information, now your risk seems calculated and can be appreciated even if/when you may fail.

Third, and maybe most importantly, is to *let the work be seen* by others. People call Elon Musk the hardest working man in his field. They never question his work ethic. No risks that he or SpaceX take are seen to be based on doing things easy or cutting corners. They are shared publicly and put on display to be measures of success and tell a story. When we hear about Elon Musk or SpaceX, we then see their failures as an integral part of their story and who they are, and why they have made it this far.

Finally, you have to be *honest about consequences*. If you fail, and the risk doesn't work, there are going to be consequences. Every time we take a step in one direction it's preventing us from taking steps down other paths. Be open with your team, colleagues, and students about the consequences of taking a risk. However, failing doesn't always bring with it negative consequences: some of the best learning experiences happen when we fail. Much of the learning comes from the process, not the end result.

Margie Warrell, author of *Stop Playing Safe*,[5] has listed these questions as a place to start when we begin to decide whether or not to take a leap of faith and try something new:

- ◆ Do I keep doing what's always been done, or challenge old assumptions and try new approaches to problems?
- ◆ Do I proactively seek new challenges or just manage those I already have?
- ◆ Do I risk being exposed and vulnerable, or act to protect my pride and patch of power?
- ◆ Do I ask for what I really want, or just for what I think others want to give me?
- ◆ Do I "toot my horn"[6] to ensure others know what I'm capable of, or just hope my efforts will be noticed?
- ◆ Do I speak my mind or bite my lip, lest I ruffle feathers or subject myself to criticism?

Ultimately, we can learn a lot from the experiences (and failures) of people like Elon Musk. Yet it comes down to our beliefs, and whether we truly think something is important enough to take a risk and possibly end up as a failure.

For me, I know that celebrating failure is hard to do. So maybe we shouldn't celebrate the failure, but instead celebrate the act of taking the risk and bouncing back, regardless of the outcome.

Here's to trying new things, being passionate about your work, and taking risks in the future that will benefit all our students—in the present and in the future.

Notes

1 http://ajjuliani.com/the-launch-cycle-a-design-thinking-framework-for-k-12-students.
2 Read this 30,000 word article on it that I loved: http://waitbutwhy.com/2015/08/how-and-why-spacex-will-colonize-mars.html/3.
3 www.wired.com/2016/02/watch-spacexs-rocket-probably-crash-robot-boat.
4 www.farnamstreetblog.com/2011/11/what-drives-loss-aversion.
5 www.forbes.com/sites/margiewarrell/2013/04/22/is-comfort-holding-you-back/#3a5db6133d91.
6 www.youtube.com/watch?v=MV9UmvQwcKo&scrlybrkr.

Chapter Reflection

What ideas resonated with you from this chapter? Take notes, draw, brainstorm, and reflect in the space below. Share your ideas on Twitter using the hashtag #beintentional.

13

Creating Conditions for Creativity

Last year, as we were digging out of the 20 inches of snow, my kids were sledding in the backyard and hiding out in their igloo. My 4-year-old son had another snow day passion: filling up a plastic cup with snow to the brim and walking around calling it his "snow cone".

He wouldn't go anywhere without his snow cone. I yelled to him, "Hey buddy, save some for the rest of us!"

He turned around, looked across the backyard and laughed. "There's enough for everyone," he said.

The next day as the temperature picked up and the snow began to melt, he came outside to see a different view and began to cry. As I asked him what was wrong, I found out he was worried the snow would all melt away and he couldn't have any more snow cones.

I consoled him for a moment (as any dad would do for his son), but then went on to explain that winter wasn't the only time you could have snow cones. I asked him, "What about in the summer, when we go down to the beach and get snow cones?"

"It doesn't snow in the summer," he said.

"I know, but all you have to have is some ice, something to shave it, and a cup. Then you've got a snow cone in any condition!"

He wasn't too sure about it, but he did remember having snow cones in the summer, and felt a bit better. He was off playing something else in the next minute, completely forgetting about his beloved snow cones.

Conditions in Our Schools and Classrooms

Later that night I couldn't help but think about the snow cone situation and how it plays out every day in schools and classrooms around the world.

We go to a conference and hear about innovative and creative work being done by high school students, but we make it about where the school is located, how they are funded, how much time they had, or who the students were. *We say that with our conditions that could never happen.*

We read an article, blog post, or book and see the innovative and creative work being done by middle school students, but we wonder who gave them the permission, how they fit that into their curriculum, and look at all of the technology they have to use. *We say that it would be nice to do that kind of work with our students, but our conditions prevent it from ever happening.*

We watch a YouTube video, or live Periscope, or webinar and see the innovative and creative work being done by elementary school students, but we ask out loud how they got their classroom to look like that, and question where the money for the supplies came from, or who came to help set all that up. *We say it looks awesome, and fun, and inspiring, but with our conditions that would be impossible.*

It's natural for us to act like my son. We think, *surely this wonderful event (whether it be snow cone or innovative work) can't happen unless the conditions are perfect!* And yet, it's about how we influence the conditions. It's how we tackle the problems and situations. It's our attitude towards the learning that often matters the most.

Our Influence Is Greater Than We Think

A recent study showed that **one simple phrase could boost student effort by 40%**:

> *I'm giving you these comments because I have very high expectations and I know that you can reach them.*

Sounds simple, right? But baked into that phrase is support, encouragement, expectations, challenge, and a human element of believing in someone else.

This type of influence was never made more apparent to me than when speaking with teacher, author, and speaker, Principal El before his TEDx talk at an event our students ran and coordinated. I asked Principal El the same question thousands of educators have over the last 10 years: "what was it like starting a chess club at an inner-city school and helping your students achieve success on an international level?" His response was similar to what was written in a recent article:

> *I started teaching special education students mathematics by using a chess-board. I demonstrated how the knights move on right angles and the bishops move on diagonals. They did a great job at grasping the concepts. So, I decided to teach every kid in the school the benefits of chess—problem solving, critical thinking, and patience. My goal for them was to become lifelong learners, not so much to become excellent chess players. I never imagined they would become national champions and go on to college, graduate school and law school! We should always follow our hopes and dreams as students and teachers. There should be no regrets . . . ever!*

I often tell my students, "Smart is not something you are, it's something you become."

We often treat our circumstances as obstacles instead of challenges. Listening to Principal El speak at TEDxPennsburgED motivated me to flip my biases and concentrate on how I could personally influence the conditions of learning in my classroom, at my school, and in our district.

Creating Conditions for Growth

Teachers and leaders around the world have grasped onto the notion of "growth" since the release of Carol Dweck's book, *Mindset*. The idea of focusing on a growth mindset instead of a fixed mindset also speaks to our roles as facilitators of student growth.

I love this quote by Sir Ken Robinson on teachers as gardeners:

> *The living process of education is one where conditions have to be influenced, molded, and supported in order for growth to sprout up. Still, we've all seen circumstances where plants grow in the cracks of a sidewalk, this is a great analogy to the forcefulness and power of learning. Certain conditions help it to grow, but learners have the ability to grow in a wide variety of conditions.*

When we talk about the notion of creativity and innovation in our schools and classrooms, are we looking at the conditions we help create and influence? Are we more worried about getting students to a certain destination, or allowing them to find their own way, with support and guidance?

Creating Intentional Conditions for Innovation

There are *four* specific ways that, as teachers and leaders, we can influence the conditions for innovation in our schools and classrooms. Each of these areas have limitations; we are bound by some constraints put forth by our state and local governments, and other measures that must be met. However, just as the gardener does not get to pick and choose when the sun comes out, we can spend a whole lot of our time worrying about the things we can't control, or start focusing on the things we can influence.

I believe in intentional innovation. A process where our actions and attitude leads to innovative work. It's not about having the ideas, it's about empowering ideas. It's not about executing our plan, it's about supporting others' work and execution. When we spend time focusing on these areas, our habits lead to innovative work and a creative mindset.

The PLASMA Framework connects the actions and intentions of the teacher to the types of learning and creating that ultimately takes place.

To truly create the conditions for this type of teaching and learning to take place, we have to build habits that foster innovation and creativity. The attitude is the mindset to try new ideas, but the action is building habits that empower students to become better at solving problems with innovative solutions.

Developing Habits That Lead to Innovation

When we look at what research says about becoming better at something, two pieces of evidence stand out.

First, we must have clarity on what our goals are and where we want to go, or what we want to become.

Second, it is deliberate practice (combined with feedback loops) that increases the myelin in our brains which, in turn, helps improve performance and growth.

I want to talk about a process that we often miss when we look at student success in the classroom. We tend to talk about growth, goals, and instructional practice . . . yet we miss a key element of going from "defining a goal" to "achieving a goal" with our students.

It's About Building Better Learning Habits

We often talk about strategies, but forget that our habits as teachers and leaders impact the habits of our students.

Students only become better at writing through deliberate practice, and feedback on that practice. But if students do not have the habit of writing every day, it is extremely difficult for them to improve that practice and reach their writing goals.

Here's where habit stacking becomes essential in our classrooms.

What Is Habit Stacking?

In S.J. Scott's book, *Habit Stacking: 97 Small Changes*,[1] he writes about the importance of habits in building towards success:

> It's been said that the average person's short-term memory can only retain seven chunks of information. So the theory behind cognitive load is that since you can only retain a small amount of information, you have to rely on long-term memory, habits and established processes to do basically everything in life.
>
> You can trace every success (or failure) in your life back to a habit. What you do on a daily basis largely determines what you'll achieve in life. Habits create routine, and let's face it—most of us run our lives by some sort of routine. We get up in the morning and follow a preset pattern: take a shower, brush our teeth, get dressed, make breakfast, drive to work, do work, and then go home. Some of us choose to follow self-improvement habits: set goals, read inspirational books, work on important projects, and ignore wasteful distractions. Others choose self-destructive habits: do the bare minimum, dull creativity through low-quality entertainment, eat junk food, and blame others for their failures in life.

That being said, we know how hard it is to try and start a new habit. Think about how many people start working out, going to the gym, and eating healthy for a New Year's Resolution. I've tried to build a habit of exercising daily multiple times in my life—only to fail multiple times!

But what I find fascinating is what I did differently when I found success. When I came up with a shared goal of running a marathon with my wife, we began to run every other day. We started with the simple act of just running; then we began to increase our distance; then we began to increase our speed. Each of these steps were incremental increases in our practice. In order to run 26 miles, we would have to start small and build our capacity. Trying to run a marathon without practice would be considered silly, but that's often what we do in schools: we ask students to do something without giving them time (and guidance) in building their capacity through practice.

Scott provides an alternative practice to building habits in his book *Habit Stacking*:

> *We all know it's not easy to add dozens of new habits to your day. But what you might not realize is it's fairly easy to build a single new routine. The essence of habit stacking is to take a series of small changes (like eating a piece of fruit or sending a loving text message to your significant other) and build a ritual that you follow on a daily basis.*
>
> *Habit stacking works because you eliminate the stress of trying to change too many things at once. Your goal is to simply focus on a single routine that only takes about 15 to 30 minutes to complete. Within this routine is a series of actions (or small changes). All you have to do is to create a checklist and follow it every single day. That's the essence of habit stacking.*

Habit stacking can be used in our classrooms and schools in a variety of ways. I've seen how a daily routine and morning meeting can get Kindergarteners ready for each day. I've noticed what a strong and daily anticipatory set (Take 5, Entrance Work, Do Now, Bell Ringer) sets students up for meaningful learning. I've witnessed teachers with communication and collaboration norms, so students understood what types of conversations were relevant to their learning.

Each of these examples can be traced back to a habit that was developed in the classroom—and each habit can help build a better practice that is connected to a learning goal.

Building Better Habits for Ourselves and Our Students

Here are 10 habits that we can start doing right now with our students.

1. Conversation at the Door/Desk
Talk to students about what's going on in their lives and they'll be more willing to come to you for help or guidance, and to take critical feedback. These short conversations spark the human and social aspect of learning that is an important piece to the puzzle. The key here is to do this with every student.

2. Take 5/Entrance Work/Do Now/Bell Ringer
When I was in college they called this the "Anticipatory Set" but who likes that name?! Traveling around the country I've heard Take 5, Entrance Work, Do Now, Bell Ringer . . . the list goes on and on. Think about your favorite TV show. Now, the next time you watch it notice how the first few minutes

are full of action and catch your attention right away. That's what the first five minutes of class should look like as well. Get 'em thinking!

3. Assess the Process of Learning

Students tend to act like the rest of us and only focus on what is being measured (graded) and praised. Make the process of learning as important as the final product (paper, project, test, etc.) and you'll see their work blossom.

4. Write Every Day

You become a better reader by writing, and become a better writer by reading. Get students (and yourself!) in the habit of writing every single day; and make it enjoyable. Use a platform like Haiku Deck with awesome visual writing prompts to spark students' imaginations.

5. Transact with Various Texts Every Day

See what I said above. It doesn't matter what subject or level you are teaching. Students need to have the daily habit of transacting with various texts (note "various"!) each day. The daily practice allows students to make connections, go into depth with analysis, and find what they truly enjoy reading.

6. Define Problems

We can't separate problem-based learning from the everyday learning that goes on in our classrooms. Make every day a problem-solving day. The first step is to define problems and empathize with the issue. When students get into the habit of defining problems to their very core, they'll look for solutions that have the biggest impact.

7. Collaboratively Work for a Solution

Collaborative work must have a reason. Sitting students in a group and having them fill out a worksheet together is not collaboration. Instead, focus on the habit of solving those problems you've defined earlier in a group type setting. This puts everyone on the same team, with the same goal.

8. Debate

Get students fired up! The idea of a daily debate was first inspired by John Spencer, and I love this in the classroom. Set norms for how to debate, talk about what makes a strong argument, and have students voice their opinions on topics they care about. When it comes time to write that paper, or give that speech, students will have a habit of making their case stand out.

9. Create/Make/Tinker/Play

It may sound obvious to get students making each day, but this is hard to do without making it a priority. I've seen too many scripted curriculum and programs that do not allow for any "tinker time" and when students finally do have this opportunity, they'd rather have a worksheet to fill out (sad, isn't it?). Do this daily and students will want to carry the making back home!

10. Reflect

We all need to reflect more. It is one of the most powerful learning tools: to self-assess and reflect on what we've learned, what we've done, and what we need to do. Have students reflect multiple times a day, and keep it short at first. This time of "taking a moment" will revitalize their minds and keep a daily practice of "thinking about thinking".

Too many habits? Start small. Try a few (or just one) in your class every day and then begin "stacking" the habits as you master the daily practice with one of them. Remember, these can also be combined in many ways/ shapes/forms, but the key is to do this daily and make it stick.

Similarly, how can we build habits with our colleagues and staff that foster the type of creativity we are hoping to see? Each habit can be connected to the praise, support, make time for, and allow areas that drive intentional innovation.

Note

1 Scott, S.J. (2014) *Habit Stacking: 97 Small Life Changes That Take Five Minutes or Less.* Florida: Archangel Ink.

Chapter Reflection

What ideas resonated with you from this chapter? Take notes, draw, brainstorm, and reflect in the space below. Share your ideas on Twitter using the hashtag #beintentional.

14

Leading the Change

When I was in high school I spent most of my time playing football and basketball, and worrying about my so-called social life. In school, I was rarely allowed to explore my interests, and thus set up a mental block against "caring" about anything academic. Even when we would do something fun or exciting in class, I would never fully allow myself to embrace the activity, or follow-up on my own time.

In this pre-Google world, if I wanted to explore an interest it would require finding (and reading) a book or article, and then possibly continuing this search online. This seemed like a lot of work to the 16–17-year-old (a bit lazy) me, so my wall stayed up and I went through the motions in school—as so many students do.

Mr. Flynn was one of my favorite teachers, and he just happened to teach one of my least favorite subjects: math. Math had never come *easily* to me the way many English and Social Studies classes had, and so I often retreated from trying and just did enough to get by. By all accounts, Mr. Flynn should never have taken an interest in my learning journey. I spent most of his Precalculus class passing notes or laughing at others, goofing around.

Then one day we came into class and Mr. Flynn was lying down on the back table. It seemed like a joke, but eventually we found out he had seriously hurt his back. He taught the rest of that class period lying on the back table, pointing to the chalkboard and using a yard stick to make changes.

Everyone thought he would be gone the next day, resting up at home, but sure enough, when we walked into class, Mr. Flynn was lying on the table again, ready to teach. There are certain moments in life where your mindset switches. I still didn't "like" Pre-calculus class, but I wasn't going to goof around any more while this teacher, in obvious pain, was coming in every day to teach instead of staying at home like so many of us would have done.

This lasted for over a month before Mr. Flynn was back up again teaching us from a standing position. One day he came over and asked me if I'd like to take computer programming the following year. He had been teaching it for a few years, but enrollment was low and he wasn't sure the class would run again. I didn't know what to say. I was shocked that he thought I would like this class but told him I'd think about it. A few days later I signed up, thinking I'd at least have a great teacher even if I didn't like the class.

I took computer programming class during my junior year. **It was so different.** I've never been a math or numbers person, but this gave numbers and formulas power. Instead of getting a "right answer" on a test for getting a formula correct, this set things in motion. We learned Pascal and Basic programming languages. It wasn't that hard, but it was challenging enough that I had to focus and pay attention during class, and could spend some extra time at night or during study hall to get better.

As a semester course, time was also limited so we had to hurry through the beginning curriculum in order to create our own projects. In my mind this is always a plus. It calls for urgency in the learning process, which makes learners and teachers more effective if they are on the same page. My final project was using this programming language to build a "football" game that looked and functioned in a similar way to the famous Nintendo Tecmo Bowl. I spent a lot of time on this—so much that I did not realize how much time I spent. In the end, my football game was not fully functional (there was no end of the game, let alone a halftime or quarter), but it had many of the same features and abilities as Tecmo Bowl. My classmates and I were able to play it. It was awesome.

I went through the rest of high school still worrying about the same things; but my outlook on learning was changed forever. When I got to college I spent more time on "side-projects" than ever before, and it lead me to become the type of learner and teacher I am today.

I tell this story, because too often we fail to let students or employees "scratch an itch". I would never have learned the math or formulas needed unless I had to program that game. It was the interest and final product that had me learning on my own time at a rapid pace. Mr. Flynn never worked to "engage" me during programming class; instead, he let the creative process fuel my work and empowered me to be a maker, instead of only a learner.

Engaging My Students

I've always remembered how Mr. Flynn's actions of going "above and beyond" engaged me as a student in his math class. It built our teacher-student relationship in ways a conversation never could. I had the ultimate respect for that man and what he brought to class every day.

In my first year of teaching at Wissahickon Middle School, I had the opportunity to work with an amazing veteran teacher—Jen Smith—who took me under her wing. One of the best things about working with Jen was her consistent goal of making the learning engaging in our classrooms. We both taught English Language Arts on the same 8th-grade team, and when we would meet to plan, Jen would often say: "so this is how we did it last year, but I want to make it better. Any way we can use technology or some other idea to make it more engaging?"

This was design thinking and innovation in action. Jen would ask for us to **Look, Listen, and Learn** (Phase 1) before we started to **Ask Questions** (Phase 2). In one particular situation, we were struggling with literary devices. We began to empathize with our students before asking questions like:

- ◆ Why would our students care about literary devices?
- ◆ What would be the best way to learn the devices?
- ◆ What would be the best way to assess their learning without regurgitation?
- ◆ How can we engage the students in understanding the devices' purpose and use in the real world?

As we answered these questions and looked at the work from previous years, we began to **Understand the Problem** (Phase 3). Literary devices had always been seen as boring. They were never presented as something exciting, just something to check off the list of having learned in 8th grade (and needed on the State standardized tests). We started to brainstorm and **Navigate Ideas** (Phase 4) on how we could teach the devices in engaging ways. One of our co-teachers offered a piece of advice: she noticed that popular songs always had literary devices in their lyrics. With that we started to **Create** (Phase 5) our very own rap song called *Welcome to Your Lit Device Education*. We had so much fun. As a team of teachers (most well into their careers) we created "Rapper names", wrote a song script with literary devices, and I used a few beats from GarageBand. Then we worked for hours **Highlighting and Fixing** the lyrics and song (Phase 6). We then recorded it and put it online.[1]

Finally, we shared it with our students (Phase 7: the **LAUNCH**) and watched as they not only laughed hysterically at us teachers, but also began to put the song on their iPods and listen to it at home. Even though I was really embarrassed at the time, it's fun to look back on this experience of solving a problem by collaborating and creating with colleagues.

Empowering Makers in My Classroom

Our students were engaged, they were focused on literary devices, but Jen wouldn't let us stop there. Our students now wanted to use programs like GarageBand, YouTube, Audacity, and others to make their own podcasts, songs, and videos.

This is the jump.

For a while, our only focus was on engaging students. We did this as teachers by making the learning meaningful, relevant, social, and human. We made connections with our students and challenged them at the right levels to see high attention and high commitment.

But when we allowed our students to make their own podcasts and songs, made time for them to create and fail along the way, supported their work, and then praised the effort and process . . . it empowered them as makers.

When our students used the design thinking process as a framework for creative work, they were not only engaged in what they were learning, but enthusiastic about what they were making for a real audience.

Are You Willing to Make the Jump?

Mr. Flynn had already won me over as a student when he taught for a month with a bad back on the table. But it was the lessons, activities, and projects we did in computer programming class that really made me appreciate him as a teacher and guide.

Similarly, our students thought we were hilarious and appreciated the time and effort we put into making our song about literary devices. But when we empowered them to make, create, and build their own podcasts and songs, the learning transformed.

My hope is that we can all have moments like Mr. Flynn, where we empower our students on top of engaging them; and ultimately that we can impact our students' lives in the same way he impacted mine—often without even knowing it happened.

Making the Jump with Technology

I've heard this question many different times, in various forms: how is technology going to save education?

Radio and TV were going to save education, but of course they didn't. They changed consumption from primarily reading or live viewing, to listening and watching—but the prediction of televisions replacing teachers in the classroom has yet to come true.

Computers and devices were going to save education. The internet was going to save education. In fact, it seems as though every time a new technology changes our way of life (radio, TV, computers, internet) we believe it is going to save education.

Let's stop thinking about technology as a cure or savior for education.

Instead let's realize that great learning experiences have always had similar patterns and pedagogical strategies, and technology can be a part of (and enhance) that experience.

Let's also stop thinking about "Ed Tech" as something that needs a massive amount of training.

Instead let's understand that teachers, students, and parents are all on different parts of the technology continuum, and will need varied support depending on their experiences. It doesn't matter if you are a digital native, digital immigrant, or digital explorer—much of how you use technology will have to be learned through actually using it, not through traditional training, because much of what you are trained on will soon change.

Let's stop believing that new tools will revolutionize education.

Instead let's understand that new tools often substitute, sometimes augment, and very rarely redefine the learning experience. It is how the teacher and students use these tools for learning that truly matters. And when technology is used to redefine a learning experience, the revolution is in what the students make, create, and build with their technology, not the many ways in which they can consume information.

What Can a New Educational Technology Narrative Look Like?

If we stop believing technology is a "savior" and start looking at it as a way to redefine learning experiences, there are a few beliefs that ring true:

1. Technology decisions should always be made with students in mind.
2. Devices should be allowed and used. In a world where much of what we do involves technology, these devices have to be allowed in school and included in the learning process.

3. Tools must have true purpose for learning (this should go beyond "spicing up" a lesson).
4. Training will have to be differentiated and unconventional (in the ever-changing world of technology our responsibility is to keep up with the world in which our students are living).
5. Technology provides new opportunities for students: global collaboration, real-time feedback, and extended learning opportunities are a few of the many ways that tech opens the door to authentic learning experiences.

Instead of focusing on how to integrate technology, schools must turn their attention to how technology has already impacted the lives of students and teachers, how it will continue to do so in the future, and what their role can be to create optimal learning experiences—in and out of the school building.

Technology is not going to save education. But it will make it different. This is a good thing.

The world in which we and our students live is so different than it was a year ago, 5 years ago, and 20 years ago. It will be different again in a year from now. How we learn will always change with the world around us, let's not let "how we teach" fall too far behind.

As technology and innovation coaches, our role is not only to help with the professional development, training, and integration involved with technology, but also to cultivate an innovative culture that does not separate technology from instruction and learning. To do that we must start with a focus on purposeful and meaningful technology use.

Note

1 https://soundcloud.com/a-j-juliani/welcome-to-your-lit-device-education.

Chapter Reflection

What ideas resonated with you from this chapter? Take notes, draw, brainstorm, and reflect in the space below. Share your ideas on Twitter using the hashtag #beintentional.

15

Innovation Starts with Passionate People

The police were on strike, yet we were still walking through the streets of Tembisa. It was the middle of July, but it wasn't hot. We were in the southern hemisphere after all, and Africa is an enormous continent. Our Western stereotypes were consistently being shattered during our visit . . .

In 2006, I took my first trip to the South African township of Tembisa, right outside of Johannesburg. I could list many different reasons why I went on this trip: I enjoyed traveling, and I had been a part of mission work before—in Guatemala, Europe, and the US. My wife (fiancée at the time) was going with me as well. So were my brothers and my sister.

All of these reasons would make sense of why we went to South Africa in the middle of summer, but they weren't the real motive. My wife and I went to Tembisa because my dad was extremely passionate about this cause. We could see how passionate he was in the way he talked about Africa and the people in Tembisa. My dad is a pastor, and the year prior he had led a small team to Swaziland (a small country landlocked inside of South Africa) and had come back to the US on fire. Our group was headed to South Africa to learn from the people there, help run a huge kids camp, and volunteer at an AIDS clinic and orphanage.

Although we spent a lot of time learning about the culture and people of South Africa, nothing could have prepared me for this experience. It changed my life in so many different ways. After a 7-hour flight to Paris, and a 11-hour flight to Johannesburg, our plane touched down and we headed towards an adventure I'd never forget.

An Early Lesson in Expectations

The scene in Tembisa was heartbreaking. The other Johannesburg township, Soweto, gets a bit more attention because of the amazing "Soweto Gospel Choir" and the Soweto Uprising in 1976[1] during Apartheid. But Tembisa has 500,000 people living in 12 square miles of makeshift buildings and dwellings. When we arrived the police were actually on strike, and civil unrest was brewing.

We stayed outside of Tembisa in "guest houses", which are a type of bed-and-breakfast in South Africa. Each day we would ride a bus into Tembisa at dawn and ride out at dusk. A light smog held over the township, and you could smell burning rubber for miles outside of the city.

Everything changed for me (and our team) when we met the group of young people we'd be working with from the local church and community center. They were teenagers, but wow, how much did I learn from them. They lived in Tembisa and were passionate about resurrecting the township and the community. They didn't let the violence, poverty, and political unrest thwart their dreams of going to college, becoming engineers, and starting their own businesses.

During the next two weeks we worked side-by-side with this group of young people to run a kids camp with over 500 kids from the township. They helped us understand their community and taught us ways to work "alongside the people" instead of working "for the people".

Interestingly, my expectation of coming to South Africa to "help" was completely biased and seemingly based on a Western perspective. Instead, we worked together. We listened. We took orders. And we relied on our friends from South Africa to show us what needed to be done, rather than coming in with an agenda of our own. In hindsight, this small change is what made the trip—and our connection and partnership ever since—so successful.

My father's passion had led me to Africa, but these teenagers' passion had led me to an understanding: **passionate individuals are the ones who create change, because they will not let the problems and issues we all see (and face) interfere with their mission.**

A Tent and Passionate People

It's now almost 8 years since that first trip to Africa. The following summer we went back, but that time to Swaziland: "infamous" for having the highest rate of HIV/AIDS in the world. We took the model of medical clinic, church, and community center (all in one building area) we saw in Tembisa and brought the idea to an area of Swaziland called Madudula.

Here our team stayed outside the city in what could only be described as a rural setting. The center was square and each of us had a room with two cement slabs to lay our sleeping bags on. No hot water. Electricity every now and then. And while the streets of Tembisa had given me a glimpse into true urban poverty, this rural poverty was a completely different way of living than most of us had ever been exposed to in our lives.

Swaziland is one of the last remaining monarchies in the world. Years after this first trip, the Queen gave our group "official" land on which to build a school, but during this time we were told by the local leaders that a valley was the perfect place to set up a medical clinic, clothes distribution, and the kid camps we were hoping to run.

So there we were, in another hemisphere, separated from the comforts of our American lives, but ready to help in any way possible, and we were asked to put up a *tent* in the middle of a valley. This was not a camping tent, as you might imagine; it was an enormous circus-type affair that took us an entire day to put up. It involved engineers guiding us on the best way to pull this monstrosity up so it would be safe for all of us to go underneath.

I learned very quickly that I was not able to take the lead on anything when it came to the tent. In fact, our group took a back seat and let the local leaders direct us on where to pull, what to hold, and how to get this thing upright and nailed into the ground. But we all worked together. We had to. There was no ego at play anywhere during this situation, because ego or planned roles would have completely ruined what we were trying to accomplish.

Innovation Does Not Have to Be New Technology

The circus tent served as a community hub for the next two weeks. And each day more and more people from the surrounding villages came down to the valley where the tent was. In hindsight I now see why this tent was so impor-tant: it was different; it represented change; and it also represented possibility.

We often think innovation has to be something new and shiny. We pair the term with people like Elon Musk who build electric cars, hyperloops, and rockets. Yet this tent was one of the most innovative things I've ever seen. But why? Because it allowed passionate people to come together for purposeful change.

The best part of this experience was that the group of teenagers from Tembisa made the trip with us. Their passion continued to impact our work and helped create lasting change in Swaziland. They could have focused on their hometown of Tembisa, yet they came to Swaziland any-way. They came to serve and were happy about it. They used the tent as a way to connect with the people there, learn their language, play games, and teach their children, showing me the power of a relentless desire to make things better.

When I look back on this trip to Swaziland, I don't remember how hard it was. Instead I remember how rewarding it was to be part of some-thing much bigger than myself. I was mostly a quiet helper, which is very different from how I am in my life at home. But it taught me some truly valuable lessons:

1. Having a serving mentality is powerful.
2. Innovation is about the impact, not just about the tool or "new thing".
3. Passionate people are making change all around this world.

My dad has since gone over to Swaziland almost 20 times. He runs Swaziland Relief,[2] which is the organization that evolved out of this trip.

Swaziland Relief has partnered with the people of Swaziland to build a community center in Madudula. Over the years they've brought much needed clothing items and medical supplies,[3] and have mobile medical clinics around the country.

The tent lasted for a couple of years. It stood the test of mother nature, and was eventually replaced (in the exact same spot) by a large community building. A well was dug and built in Madudula and we now have a six-classroom school for grades 1–3 that serves 150 children all year long; it also has plans for expansion of one new grade level each year!

I've seen first-hand the impact passionate people can have, which is why I've been such an advocate for passion and purpose-driven learning in our schools.

> *Never depend upon institutions or government to solve any problem. All social movements are founded by, guided by, motivated, and seen through by the passion of individuals.*
>
> —Margaret Mead[4]

I will never forget that tent. But more importantly, I won't forget what it represented, and how the people of Madudula grew it to be a space where people learn and help each other every single day. Let's not forget that inno-vation is not always the brightest, newest piece of technology—it can be something that represents change, allows people to grow, and supports a cause worth working towards.

Back to the First Principles of Learning

In the opening of this book we took a hard look at the first principles of teaching and learning: how we learn, why we learn, and how the changing world is impacting what is happening in our schools and classrooms.

When we start with the first principles, we can build on those blocks for innovative ways to teach and learn.

Learning starts with paying attention. It's almost impossible to learn if you aren't doing this. And whenever you are paying attention, this has the ability to turn into learning.

Attention happens for two reasons: necessity and interest. Nature uses necessity to drive quick learning feedback loops. When we try to manufacture necessity (think: you must learn this because of a pop quiz tomorrow), a culture of compliance follows. When we allow for interest to drive attention, commitment to the learning process follows.

Relationships directly impact attention, and therefore, learning.

Learning happens inside our head. Understanding is demonstrated outside our head.

Technology is a byproduct of "learning + creativity": both must be present for technology to exist.

Learning has nothing to do with innovation. But innovation has everything to do with learning.

Intrinsic motivation will always outperform extrinsic motivation when it comes to learning.

Worms are better than strawberries and cream. As Dale Carnegie said:

> Personally I am very fond of strawberries and cream, but I have found that for some strange reason, fish prefer worms. So when I went fishing, I didn't think about what I wanted. I thought about what they wanted. I didn't bait the hook with strawberries and cream. Rather, I dangled a worm or grasshopper in front of the fish and said: "Wouldn't you like to have that?"

I believe this to be exceptionally true when thinking about engaging and empowering our students. What do they prefer? Start with that.

Learning doesn't have to be meaningful and relevant. But relevant learning experiences draw students in, and meaningful learning experiences stick with them. If you have the choice to make learning meaningful and relevant, you should go the extra mile every time.

Learning is wild. It's messy. It's free.

What's the Best That Could Happen?

My first season as a head football coach, our team had gone undefeated leading up to the final game of the season. We had a heck of a team with two great running backs, a stout defense, and a quarterback who completely understood our offense.

Somehow the scene was set up out of a teen movie. Our final game of the season was our only night game under the lights on a turf-field. The team we were going up against was also undefeated. To say the kids were excited would be an enormous understatement—they were jacked up!

And then, a day before the game, my starting quarterback was diagnosed with mono. He could not practice or play. That was it. We were doomed.

I had a few players who took snaps at quarterback, but none of them could throw the ball that well, and I had failed as a coach to prepare for this to happen. I talked with my assistant coaches and we decided to start our backup QB (a younger player). His job would be to hand off the ball to our star running backs. We also decided our backup QB for the game would be our middle linebacker (he had previously played offensive line) and asked him to learn some of the plays the night before, and on the day of the game.

The game started and we immediately had problems on offense. We ran a play the wrong way. Their defensive line stopped our running backs in the backfield. We had a small chance of winning this game (or even scoring a point) in my mind. You could see it in our player's faces: this was a different level of team that we were playing.

At this point we had a decision to make: keep trying what wasn't working, or make a change and see what would happen.

If we kept the QB the same, maybe we could break a long run and score. Our defense was playing well so maybe they could score on a turnover. After the first quarter I called my coaches together.

"What about changing up the QB? We need to make a change . . ." I said.

My assistant coach replied, "What's the worst that can happen?"

I thought to myself . . . a lot could go wrong if we do this, we might end up losing by 30 points if things started falling apart.

And then my assistant coach said, "I mean, what's the best that could happen? It's not like we have many other options . . . it's keep doing what we are doing . . . or change it up!"

We spend a lot of time worrying about what's the "worst" that could happen. We do this in our jobs, in our life, and in our relationships.

This isn't a "glass half full, or half empty" type of issue. This is more like our default self-preservation settings. We do not like making decisions that have a possibility of risk. Even if the reward for making that decision could outweigh the risk.

That game we put in our middle linebacker as our quarterback. We won 23–0. He scored all three of the touchdowns, and man I couldn't believe how amazingly he performed—which in turn impacted our entire team.

Looking back on that decision, it was one of those times that I asked, "What's the best that could happen?" instead of thinking about the risk and what could go wrong.

In the past couple of years, I've begun to ask that question with many of my decisions. And this may sound cheesy, but it works.

When you're optimistic without any understanding of risk, then you sound crazy. But when you share a positive outlook on a situation, while acknowledging what could go wrong, it shows that you understand what is at stake, and choose to believe.

I took the time when I turned 30 to look at the goals I had for myself, and wrote down all the amazing things that have happened in my life so far. I plan on doing that every year (and maybe every month) to remind me of the good things, and why it is important to believe the best can happen.

I'd challenge you to start reframing opportunities and situations with this mindset, and see what happens:

◆ Are we asking what's the best that could happen with each student?
◆ Are we asking what's the best that could happen with our team, or teachers?
◆ Are we asking what choices we can make to grow and build, even if it comes with some risk involved?

Don't get me wrong. There are days when I'm negative, and wonder if anything is going to work out the way I hoped and planned it would, but the next day always brings new possibilities. I have to remember that most of the good things in my life did not go according to plan. They happened because I was open to trying something new, something different, and focusing on the best that could happen.

Notes

1 http://en.wikipedia.org/wiki/Soweto.
2 http://swazilandrelief.org.
3 http://swazilandrelief.org/relief-supplies-sea-container.
4 www.goodreads.com/author/show/61107.Margaret_Mead.

Chapter Reflection

What ideas resonated with you from this chapter? Take notes, draw, brainstorm, and reflect in the space below. Share your ideas on Twitter using the hashtag #beintentional.

Made in the USA
Las Vegas, NV
12 October 2021